PLATO AND AUGUSTINE

KARL JASPERS

PLATO

AND

AUGUSTINE

EDITED BY HANNAH ARENDT

TRANSLATED BY RALPH MANHEIM

A Harvest/HBJ Book
A Helen and Kurt Wolff Book
Harcourt Brace Jovanovich, Publishers
San Diego New York London

ISBN 0-15-672035-3 (Harvest/HBJ : pbk.)

Originally published in German as part of
Die grossen Philosophen I
by R. Piper & Co. Verlag, München, 1957

Printed in the United States of America
E F G H I J

Acknowledgments

Acknowledgment is made for permission to use the following: For the quotations from Plato: *Protagoras and Meno,* trans. by W. K. C. Guthrie, Penguin Books, Penguin Classics #L68; *The Symposium,* trans. by W. Hamilton, Penguin Books, Penguin Classics #L24; *Euthyphro, Crito, Apology and Symposium,* trans. by Benjamin Jowett, rev. by Moses Hadas, copyrighted, reprinted with the permission of the Henry Regnery Company, Chicago, 1953 (Gateway Edition); *The Republic of Plato,* trans. with Introduction and Notes by Francis Macdonald Cornford, Oxford University Press; *Plato's Theory of Knowledge: the Theaetetus and the Sophist of Plato,* trans. by Francis Macdonald Cornford, Liberal Arts Library, London, Routledge & Kegan Paul Ltd. For the quotations from *The Confessions of Saint Augustine* in the translation of F. J. Sheed, copyright 1943, Sheed & Ward, Inc., New York; *Basic Writings of St. Augustine,* ed. by Whitney J. Oates, Vol. 1, *Confessions,* trans. by J. G. Pilkington, 1948, Random House, Inc., and T. & T. Clark, Edinburgh

CONTENTS

PLATO AND AUGUSTINE

PLATO

The enormous amount of philological and philosophical investigation devoted to Plato has produced agreement on matters of external fact, but not on the questions fundamental to an understanding of this philosopher. The difficulty lies in the nature of the matter, namely philosophy itself: Plato was a founder; only beginning with him can we speak of philosophy in the full sense of the word. To understand Plato means not to measure him by a preconceived notion of philosophy, but rather, regardless of whether we follow him or move in an entirely different direction, to take him as a basis for testing our own thinking as well as the philosophy that came after him.

I. LIFE, WORKS, THE PREREQUISITES FOR AN UNDERSTANDING OF PLATO

1. *Life* (428-347 B.C.)

Plato came from the high Athenian aristocracy. His mother's family traced its descent to Solon's brother, his father's legendary genealogy went back to King Codrus. He was profoundly attached to Athens, the polis that had produced Solon's legislation, defeated the Persians, saved freedom, created the tragedy, and built the Acropolis. His origins gave him the sovereign ease and freedom of mind that tend to make us overlook the severe discipline of an infinitely laborious life.

At the age of twenty, Plato, the aristocrat, became a follower of Socrates, the artisan's son. Little is known of their association, which continued to the time of Socrates' death (408-399 B.C.).

When Plato was forty years of age (c. 389-388), he visited southern Italy and Sicily. In Italy he became acquainted with the Pythagoreans; in Syracuse he met the tyrant Dionysius I and won the friendship of his brother-in-law Dion, then a youth of twenty, who became a devoted follower of Plato and his philosophy. On his return to Athens (c. 388) Plato founded the Academy. In 368, when he was sixty, Aristotle, then a young man of twenty, joined the Academy (and belonged to it for twenty years, until Plato's death in 347).

In 367 Dionysius I died. His son Dionysius II and Dion invited Plato to Syracuse. The tyrant had resolved to build a new state in collaboration with the philosopher, who saw a wonderful opportunity to put his political ideas into practice. His dealings with Dionysius (366–365) were unsuccessful. But five years later, Plato once again let himself be tempted (361–360), and again the enterprise ended badly. These two ventures occurred when Plato was sixty-two and sixty-seven. Some years later Dion raised an army, drove the tyrant from Syracuse, and determined once again to establish Plato's republic. Dion was murdered in 354 when Plato was seventy-four. His deepest friendships had been with Socrates, forty years older than himself, and with Dion, who was twenty years younger. After the loss of Dion he lived another seven years.

Plato was born one year after the death of Pericles; as a child and young man he experienced the downfall of Athens, the alternation of parties and forms of government, the disastrous political turmoil. His life was situated in the period before the turn from the polis to the empire, from the Greek to the Hellenistic world. He saw the ruin but did not see or foresee the other, new world. In this situation the young man, spurred on by his family tradition, was passionately drawn to political life. But he recognized the hopelessness of the situation. After the death of Socrates he made the radical decision to withdraw from public life and live for philosophy, though prepared at any moment to answer a call in a new situation. All this is known to us from his own testimony, for after the murder of Dion he wrote a deeply moving letter to Dion's friends (*The Seventh Letter*). This is the only source of any reliable insight into Plato's life. The letter is a balance sheet of his political experience. He tells how in his youth politics brought him disappointment on disappointment. In Athens after the catastrophe, the oligarchy of the nobles (404) proved so lawless and unjust that the former democracy seemed like pure gold by comparison; Plato refused to participate. The restored democracy (403) seemed to offer him an opportunity. But it was this democracy that condemned Socrates to death.

At last I perceived that the constitution of all existing states is bad and their institutions all past' remedy without a combination of radical measures and fortunate circumstance; and I was driven to affirm, in praise of true philosophy, that only from the standpoint of such philosophy was it possible to take a correct view of public and private right, and that accordingly the human race would never see the end of trouble until true lovers of wisdom should come to hold political power, or the holders of political power should, by some divine appointment, become lovers of wisdom.[1]

Where an opportunity seemed to offer itself (in Syracuse), Plato boldly undertook political experiments. But he accepted no compromise. He wished to put true order into the whole of a polis. He refused to content himself,

[1] *Seventh Letter,* 326 a-b, *The Republic,* tr. F. M. Cornford, p. xxv.

merely for the sake of playing a part, with "the best that is possible under the circumstances." He wanted everything or nothing. He demanded a kind of politics that would mold true men and so lay the foundations of a human ethos. All his life Plato reflected on politics. The greatest work of his mature age is concerned with the state; his most extensive work, completed in his old age, deals with the laws. But passionately as he thought about politics, he did not regard it as the ultimate. The ultimate, he believed, can be touched upon only through pure philosophy.

2. *Works*

The philological efforts of a century have classified and arranged the writings of Plato as handed down from antiquity in the *corpus platonicum,* and established reliable texts. After extraordinary fluctuations of opinion, scholars are pretty well agreed as to which texts are authentic and the order in which they were written.[2]

The following chronological sequence is generally accepted, though there is some doubt about the order within the groups: 1. The trial of Socrates: *Apology, Crito.* Early dialogues: *Protagoras, Ion, Laches, Lysis, Charmides, Euthyphro, Greater Hippias.* 2. After the first journey in 388 and the founding of the Academy, probably: *Gorgias, Meno, Euthydemus, Cratylus;* certainly: *Symposium, Phaedo, Republic, Theaetetus.* 3. After the second journey of 366: *Parmenides, Sophist, Statesman, Philebus, Phaedrus.* 4. After the third journey in 361: *Timaeus, Critias, Laws, Seventh Letter.*

Each group has its distinct character.

Apology and *Crito,* dealing with the trial of Socrates, are in a class by themselves. The early "Socratic" dialogues are distinguished by the uncommon vividness of the scene in which they are set (though this quality occurs in some of the later dialogues, particularly *Phaedrus,* where it attains its utmost perfection). In content, they are characterized by aporias: the main questions are left open. In the ensuing dialogues, particularly *Gorgias* and *Meno,* Plato's characteristic manner of thinking is already at work. The classical works, *Symposium, Phaedo, Republic,* reflect Plato's philosophy with its well-balanced themes, its wealth of reference, its profound conception of the One. Dialectic becomes dominant in *Theaetetus, Parmenides, Sophist, Statesman, Philebus. Phaedrus* is unique, combining youthful freshness and a perfect philosophical maturity. This is the work that has most often changed its chronological position; formerly regarded as early, today it is assigned to Plato's old age and regarded by some as one of the very latest

---

[2] Some of the spurious dialogues have a certain importance. They reflect a spirit which tried, under a variety of forms, to gain recognition in the Academy. It is instructive to contrast the authentic works with certain of them, particularly those which reveal a didactic clarity, a lyric enthusiasm, a rational skepticism, a narrow radicalism, or a tendency to devise legends. They bring out Plato's unequaled stature and give us a deeper understanding of him.

dialogues. In the late works, *Timaeus, Critias, Laws,* the dialogue form gives way to exposition.

From the standpoint of content, the dialogues may be grouped roughly as follows: The person of Socrates: *Euthyphro, Apology, Crito, Phaedo, Protagoras;* the fully developed idea of Socrates: *Symposium, Phaedrus.* Dialectics: *Parmenides, Sophist, Statesman, Theaetetus, Philebus,* sixth and seventh books of *Republic;* in the earlier dialogues: *Cratylus, Euthydemus, Meno.* The cosmos: *Timaeus, Phaedo, Philebus.* Mathematics: *Meno, Republic.*

It is interesting to note the preference given to certain dialogues and groups of dialogues at different times: In late antiquity and the Middle Ages, first place was accorded to the *Timaeus* with its discussion of the creation and structure of the cosmos. Beginning with late antiquity, the *Parmenides* was interpreted as theology and enjoyed a favored position for this reason. The most moving and living dialogues have always been *Phaedo,* the book that taught men how to die; *Apology* and *Crito* with their portrait of Socrates, the steadfast, independent man, who by his death bears witness to the truth; *Symposium* and *Phaedrus,* which show Socrates as he lived in the world, a man intoxicated with the Eros; *Gorgias,* which uncompromisingly states the alternative of good or evil. The political dialogues, *Republic, Statesman, Laws* captivate us by the earnestness with which they approach the fundamental question of our social existence as a condition of man's being. Today, the "logical" dialogues, *Theaetetus, Parmenides, Sophist, Philebus,* have entered the forefront of interest.

If we are to know the whole Plato, we cannot disregard a single dialogue. Of course there are "principal works." But each of the others throws an indispensable light on something of importance. And in spite of what they lose in translation, all are beautiful.

3. Foundations of an Understanding of Plato

A. *How shall we interpret Plato?* Interpretation begins with *individual* dialogues. We consider each one as a whole, as an exposition of ideas and as a work of art. We take thematically similar passages from other dialogues and compare the structure, scenery, characters. It may seem barbarous to dismember such works of art. But each dialogue points beyond itself; its meaning drives us to the others. To understand it we must understand all the dialogues and understand each one as a part of the whole.

Then we consider the work in its entirety, proceeding on the assumption that Platonic thinking is a system or is developing in the direction of a system like that of Aristotle and many other philosophers. Unfortunately, Plato did not expound this system. It lies embedded in the dialogues, mingled with "poetry" and always accompanied by digressions. We presume that

Plato's system was formulated in his academic lectures, which unlike those of Aristotle have not been preserved. Aristotle's notes may permit us to reconstruct the content of the lectures, at least those of Plato's later years. On the basis of this assumed system, we now approach the dialogues as quarries from which we draw the blocks for a systematic edifice: Plato's system in the form of a comprehensive doctrine (Zeller). In this process we encounter one difficulty after another. We rebel against the absurdity of destroying existing structures for the sake of a rational system that can never be anything but imaginary. The building does not advance, because once we resolve to fit each idea into its proper place in a rational totality, we run into contradiction.

Everyone will agree that the fifty years of Plato's thinking and writing must be viewed as a continuous whole. But the question remains: In what sense is it a whole? The very earliest dialogues are masterpieces, unexcelled in their kind. Proceeding from work to work, we find development, an increasing breadth and richness, but no abrupt leaps. The one revolution in Plato's thinking was brought about by Socrates and occurred *before* any of the extant works were written. The dialogues show no sudden advance that might have left a fissure in the groundwork of his philosophizing. But though there is no explicit system and no indication of the stages of Plato's development, wholeness must be seen in something which pervades the entire work and defies exact formulation, namely philosophizing itself, the continuous, never-ending process wherein the true is manifested. Doctrine and system are a part of it, systematic relations are its instruments, but there is no one system that it employs exclusively. Plato is always master of his tools.

In our effort to explore Plato's philosophizing, one task will lead us to another. The first step must be to interpret the problems discussed in the texts. Each dialogue has its questions and themes. They deal with logic, politics, physics, cosmology, in short, almost every aspect of the world and of human existence. We reflect on what Plato puts into the mouth of his characters, isolate the self-contained discussions of particular philosophical themes, and consider the timeless problems involved. From other dialogues, we borrow related subject matter that may either complement or contradict the passage we are studying. We effect a critique of Plato's ideas by examining the themes themselves in order to see what they show independently of Plato.

The contradictions, in particular, may help to call our attention to Plato's central meaning. Of course the problems he treats are important in themselves, and of course they were of the deepest interest to Plato. The philosophical mind, in any case, can only communicate itself through the themes of philosophy; they cannot be set aside as irrelevant. But we must go on to ask the essential question: How do they relate to the whole, what is their function, what do they mean, directly or indirectly? Since it has not been possible to construe them as fragments that can be assembled into an encompassing rational system, let us approach them as elements of an infinitely mobile philosophizing that utilizes the thematic problems only as a language in which to express something else.

We begin by looking for this something else in the characters who philosophize in Plato's dialogues, first in the unique Socrates who towers above them all, then in the others. They are not mere mouthpieces for the discussion of philosophical problems, but are characterized as living philosophical or unphilosophical realities by the way in which they speak, their conduct in the situations of the dialogues, their reactions and responses. They are portraits not so much of a psychology as of an intellectual mood. In the most significant passages, they are spiritual forces that meet in personal form. The philosophical problems acquire truth only by being taken into the encompassing truth, and it is from the vantage point of this encompassing truth that they first arouse our interest.

If the full truth is attained neither by a discussion of the contents nor by an investigation of the personal figures in their agreements and conflicts, we must take a further step. Plato guides our attention to something that cannot be understood or demonstrated by reason, something that is not analyzed but merely narrated, namely the myths. Despite the rationalist critics who regard these myths as superfluous, Plato clearly attaches great importance to them. We are led for a moment to hope that they will reveal the ultimate secret of Platonic truth. But in vain, for Plato expressly gives his myths a "playful" character.

Each of our three steps, interpretation of the philosophical problems, interpretation of the living characters, and interpretation of the myths, presupposes a distinct view of philosophy: as doctrine, as a form of personal life, as a kind of poetry. Each of these interpretations is justified insofar as it elucidates something in Plato's work. But they all fail if taken as means of penetrating Plato's philosophy as a whole. The systematization of the ideas involves us in discrepancies and contradictions. The characters are figures through which Plato indirectly expresses the truth; they are not the truth itself, for none of them, not even Socrates, is always right. The poetic interpretation is encouraged by the possibility of taking Plato's dialogues as poems (setting aside the intellectual difficulties); it is supported by the theory that from the standpoint of cultural history Plato is a successor of the tragic and comic writers, that he himself wrote tragedies in his youth and burned them when Socrates led him to take a new step in his quest for the truth, a step that went beyond poetry. But the new step carried him into the realm of thinking. We must find out what thinking is in Plato.

Thus the study of Plato requires us to learn what philosophy can be; not to presuppose what philosophy is, but to investigate the nature of Plato's philosophizing in its historical envelope; to discover what insuperably great thing happened, what it was that provided Western philosophy with a definitive foundation, whose manifold meanings are perhaps inexhaustible.

This high estimate of Plato involves a methodological conclusion that is applicable to very few philosophers: namely, that nothing in the texts can be neglected as unimportant, that everything must have meaning in a context of philosophical communication, that nothing can be considered from a merely aesthetic or rational point of view. A related conclusion is that we must aim at the source of Plato's thinking, his thinking in *statu nascendi,* the living process from which everything springs and in the light of which all modes of communication, all themes and contents, are fragmentary. It is hoped that the themes we take up successively will guide us to the One, the realization of man in Plato's philosophizing.

But first we must briefly consider the conditions of this philosophizing, its foundation in Socrates, and its relationship to the whole pre-Socratic (better, pre-Platonic) philosophy.

B. *Plato and Socrates:* Plato's philosophy began with the overpowering impact of Socrates upon him as a young man. Socrates awakened him to the one thing that is important: to care for your soul by leading the right life oriented toward eternal being. His love of this unique man was one with his own inspiration. Plato's philosophy is grounded in a lifelong personal attachment. The fixed point in this philosophy is not nature, not the world, not man, not a problem, not a theorem, but all of these because the center upon which the whole rests is one man. To discern the nature of this attachment is one of the conditions for an understanding of Plato.

In the dialogues Plato develops his philosophy as though it were the creation of Socrates. The most original of thinkers declines to show his originality. Plato thinks, as it were, through Socrates. We do not know to what extent his own thinking is grounded in what was imparted to him in conversations with Socrates, or what thoughts which came to him in the presence of Socrates he imputed to him as a matter of course though the older philosopher had never said anything of the sort (this would seem to be the case with the theory of Ideas as set forth in the *Phaedo,* where Socrates tells how he arrived at it). We may say that what Plato first expresses is not the philosophy but the philosopher as he saw him in reality. He discloses philosophy in his presentation of the philosopher. Plato's poetic invention found the philosopher in the real man whom he knew and loved. The philosophy is stated indirectly, as though it were a part of the poem about the philosopher. But the subject of this poem is not only an individual man; it is man as such, in all the unfathomable possibility of his thinking.

Socrates would be a historical reality even without Plato. But the historical and the Platonic Socrates are inseparable. In the reality of Socrates, Plato discerned his essence. He let the essence unfold freely in his dialogues; in so doing he did not restrict himself to facts, but he was always guided by a striving for essential truth. His philosophical poetry is a picture of the essential truth of Socrates. Throughout the dialogues, Socrates, with all his many aspects, is one man. The reader always sees the one Socrates even when he is portrayed from different points of view. In most of the dialogues, Socrates is the main character; in some of the late dialogues, he becomes a secondary figure, and in *Laws* he disappears, because the subject matter no longer fits in with the individuality of Socrates.

Can poetry disclose reality? But what is objective truth in our picture of a man? Only externals can be demonstrated to the satisfaction of all. What a man really is, is inseparably reality and idea, realization and potentiality, success and failure in finding himself, the process whereby he becomes what he is. Only modern psychologists suppose that they really know the man they submit a report on. What a man is, is a light in the eyes of one who loves him; for true love is clearsighted and not blind. What Plato saw in Socrates was really Socrates—compounded of the idea, the visible embodiment, and the man who looked as Xenophon describes him.

It is not possible to draw an objective line between the ideas of Socrates and those of Plato. Where there is a personal bond between two men, that is never possible. In such cases there are no rights of ownership. Plato develops what is implicit in an idea, what can spring from a philosophical reality. Socrates-Plato is the only case in the history of philosophy of a thinker who is great only in bond with another, of two thinkers who exist through each other.

Plato's profound relation to Socrates has three main consequences for Plato's philosophy:

1. Plato built his thinking on the philosopher and not merely on an abstract, universal, free-floating truth. His presentation of the philosophy in one with the philosopher maintains a unity of thinking and existence. That is what gave Platonic thinking its enduring historical concreteness (though Plato, who had no sense of history, found the source and meaning of his philosophy in its apprehension of the universal). And it enabled Plato to do what is impossible for any thinker who merely follows out a doctrine: to think in perfect freedom while maintaining a historical bond; to venture every idea, because his ideas, sustained by a man and his living reality, would not lead him into the void. This accounts for the measure and limit in Plato, his avoidance of all philosophizing that would have led to mere universals. But, what is most astonishing in all this, the person of Socrates is not dogmatized. Love was no check on freedom. Plato's thinking was subservient neither to a fixated doctrine nor to an idolized man, but only to a spirit of endlessly burgeoning discovery rooted in human companionship.

2. This method of thinking exempted Plato, in certain situations, from the need to set his name to statements that he might not have ventured on his own authority. He lets the transfigured Socrates say these things, just as Socrates, beyond certain limits, lets others speak, Diotima or the narrator of the myths. With this device Plato seems to be saying: The claims of philosophy are so great that I should not dare to call myself a philosopher.

He is better prepared to love and portray the philosopher in another man. (We are reminded that Kant, too, was reluctant to call himself a philosopher.)

3. The Socrates-Plato relationship does away with the isolation of the individual. Monologue, aloneness, the thinker's reliance on himself makes all truth questionable. "Truth begins with two" (Nietzsche). To become himself the individual needs the other. To place his trust in the other is man's first act of selfhood.

This duality and unity of Socrates-Plato is something that only happened once in the history of philosophy, but the truth it embodies is all-encompassing. Though never repeated, it is echoed in all philosophizing: Love of the great man, love of one man has given men the courage to philosophize. Usually the love is anonymous, but the memory of this situation runs through the history of philosophy. Socrates and Plato are an archetype. Perhaps every young man is looking for a Socrates. Perhaps he does not dare to philosophize in his own name, but "invents" the philosopher in the best man or men he has met in his life (and such true poetic invention is a revelation of reality). And, by contrast, what a forbidding atmosphere, what a false light, where thought ceases to be accompanied by communication and where doctrines passed on without communication become pedantic phrases and literary affectations.

Socrates and Plato are not a repetition of the same thing; they are utterly different. Although it is hard to form a historical picture of Socrates, while Plato's historic reality is established, the two realities are comparable. In his reaction to Socrates and portrayal of Socrates, Plato, in collaboration with Socrates, brought forth philosophy as an objective work. The death of Socrates led Plato to profound insight, but it also made it clear to him that he himself would have to take a path different from that of Socrates. In the fulfillment of the task appointed him by the Godhead, Socrates, at the end, did not shrink from provoking hatred; he became a martyr. Plato was not prepared to die in this way. Socrates was always in the streets of Athens; Plato, by design, lived in retirement and turned his back on a present that he regarded as evil. He says as much in the *Republic*: In bad times hide, take shelter until the storm and the rain have passed. Socrates was bound to Athens; Plato remained an Athenian but was on his way to becoming a cosmopolitan; he was capable of living and working outside of his native city. Socrates philosophized in the immediate present, Plato indirectly, through his works and the school he founded. Socrates remained in the market place, Plato withdrew to the Academy with a chosen few. Socrates did not write a line, Plato left a monumental written work.

c. *The importance of the traditional philosophy for Plato:* The themes of Plato's philosophizing are those of the older Greek philosophers and of his contemporaries. All previous Greek ideas, flowing independently from many sources, seem to have gathered in Plato's all-encompassing mind. But here the sources fuse together, because they are taken into a new realm of meaning. Of course, when we study Plato we do not keep glancing backward and to the side. Nevertheless, we must be aware of the dependencies and their significance.

Plato progressively mastered the whole philosophical tradition: the cosmology of the Miletus philosophers (Thales, Anaximander, Anaximenes), of Anaxagoras and Empedocles; he was comforted with the ethos of the Greek aristocracy and with that of the Seven Wise Men; he knew Heraclitus and Parmenides with their still valid elucidations of being; the philosophers who rejected the myths as an insult to the gods and Xenophanes' idea of the One God; the Orphic-Pythagorean doctrines of the soul, immortality, and transmigration; the beginnings of scientific geography and medicine, and the vast discoveries of Plato's contemporaries in mathematics and astronomy; the intellectual radicalism of the Sophist period, the investigation of logic. All this is essential to an understanding of Plato, the source of his richness. The cosmologies and faiths, the attempts at methodic thought, the emerging personalities of the thinkers, the natural forces and human situations that had entered into men's awareness, the innumerable problems that had made their appearance—Plato made all this his own and transformed it.

Plato once said of the traditional ideas: everything these thinkers said is fairy tales (*mythoi*) told to children. The one says this, the other something else, without foundation: being is threefold; there is conflict and, again, there is love; there are two elements, moist and dry, hot and cold, and so on; everything is one; being is many and one. But with all this they talk over our heads. Heedless of whether or not we can follow and keep up with their disquisitions, each one carries out his own argument. In every case it is questionable whether we understand the meaning of the words. In all this it is hard to decide whether one of them is right or not.

These themes spurred Plato to thought. He interprets them, puts them in motion; they take on a new meaning and all together enter into a state of suspension. In Plato we find these traditional ideas, sometimes with names, sometimes without. Among other things, Plato's dialogues are a source for pre-Platonic philosophy.

Plato's manner of recasting the old ideas was not that of the great synthetic mind that combines everything in a universal edifice. His way was to penetrate more deeply, not into themes that were already known, but into thinking itself and only thereby into the themes. Plato raised the traditional ideas from reality to potentiality. With him they ceased to be palpable and exclusive.

Before Plato there was a poetic expression of the world. There was an experience of sequences of phenomena in nature and human life, and there were proverbs. There was the objectivizing knowledge which no longer looked at things according to an analogy of personal action (myths) but according to a new, mechanical kind of analogy (e.g., the conception of the stars as holes in the bowl of heaven, through which the outer fire shines, or the interpretation of things as consequences of the pressure and impact of tiny indivisible particles). There were a number of schematic and mutually contradictory systems of total knowledge. Plato recast these and other forms of knowledge without sacrificing their limited meaning. By looking at them from a distance, he absorbed them into ideas that went beyond them. He transformed them into experiments and so set them in motion. He cast off the fetters which bind all thought that is uttered as though the thought were being itself. And he cast off the fetters that fixed ideas are always trying to impose on us.

By thus setting himself free, he made possible an inner action in thought and for the first time gave thought its existential efficacy. By the freedom with which he handled all the possible contents of thought, he attained to a fundamental thinking, to thinking itself, which, though communicable only through the medium of the themes within its reach, does not allow them to draw it into new captivities.

With Plato's method, truth itself took on a new character. It ceased to be a content of discourse, an object of intuition, imprisoned in statement, assertion, language as such. Up until then this had been the situation in philosophy and by his awareness of it Plato became free as no one before him. Magnificent as pre-Platonic philosophy is with its monumental structures, its closeness to the source, the endless interpretations to which it gives rise—we can admire it but not enter into it. For in their radicality these philosophies are like a set of new prejudices. Despite the Romantic longing with which one may look back at this lost world of primordial revelation, one may well utter a sigh of relief on coming to Plato from the pre-Socratics.

II. THE PLATONIC PHILOSOPHY

The Platonic philosophy can be described in its doctrines: the theory of Ideas, the idea of God, the doctrine of the soul, the political projects, the idea of the cosmos. In each case we find a comprehensive totality, and all these totalities are interrelated. But in order to arrive at the source from which all this derives its meaning, we must adumbrate the new thinking inspired by Socrates. It is there that we discern the impulsion, unexhausted to this day, which is the true power of Platonic thinking. It is therein—and not in any doctrines, systems, personal portraits—that the Platonists of the centuries are united, though to this day none of them has ever been able to say what it actually is. We shall attempt to give an idea of it under the heads: *Platonic Thinking; The Question of Communicability; Idea, Dialectic, Eros.*

1. *Platonic Thinking*

A. *The early dialogues:* These dialogues, still very close to the living Socrates, present the secret of clear thinking in an investigation of the question of *aretē* (virtue, excellence): What is it? Can it be taught? Is it knowledge? Is it one or manifold?

All the early dialogues circle around this one theme, which springs from "concern for the soul." The fundamental concept of *aretē* was inherent in the Greek view of the world. The word applies to all excellence, that of things, but particularly that of men. It refers to the radiance of an excellence that shows itself in contest, the particular *aretē* of the man, the woman, the ages of life. There is the ethical *aretē,* which relates to being and to what men ought to do, to the particular qualities of justice, courage, wisdom, prudence, piety, magnanimity, and to the epitome of all *aretai*. There is both a civil and an individual *aretē*. To the area of these meanings belong Platonic propositions such as: The *aretē* of each thing consists in that whereby it fulfills its task.

The Sophists claimed to teach *aretē*, particularly of the political sort. They aspired to teach men how to achieve success and power. Socrates, on the contrary, contends that for each activity, for farming, navigation, shoemaking, carpentry, and so on, it is best to choose an expert. If you want someone to learn a particular thing, send him to such an expert. But who is expert in education, in *aretē* as a whole, or in political matters? In other words, who is expert in what is most important of all? Clearly many *aretai* can be taught. But the most important cannot, as is evident from the fact that the great and successful, those men who are rich in the *aretē* that applies to matters of state, cannot teach their own sons; that discerning citizens cannot communicate their *aretē* to others.

If *aretē* can be taught, it must be a knowledge. But certain *aretai,* such as courage, are innate and have nothing to do with knowledge. Others, those of craftsmen for example, can be acquired by practice. If there is a knowledge of *aretē*, it should further be distinguished whether this knowledge is a means by which to attain *aretē*, or whether there is a knowledge which is itself *aretē,* so that in this case, *aretē* is knowledge and knowledge itself is the being of him who acts well. Such knowledge cannot be taught in the same way as the knowledge that is a means to an end. Where the latter suffices, the Sophists are not wrong. But the other knowledge is on an entirely different plane and the problem of imparting it is of an entirely different nature. What Plato seeks is this knowledge which is not a means to something else, but itself an end and perfection, this knowledge which is the actuality of thinking action, of man himself.

Or to say the same thing in a different form: We know something, we know how to do something (*technē*), we have many particular knowledges of this kind. The question then arises: What is the purpose of this knowledge and the achievement it confers? For the whole can be employed well and badly. Everything depends on another knowledge that supplies the answer to the question: "Good for what?" and answers it in such a way that no additional questioning is possible, because the good itself stands before our eyes. In this knowledge the ultimate authority is present. It supplies the answer to the questions: On what ground, in the service of whom or what, in view of what, is something good, not in relation to something else but in itself? This fundamental idea is simple in form; it is infinitely important, and so difficult to carry through that it crops up time and time again in Plato, and is never brought to a complete and final solution.

In the early dialogues it is stated in different variants, as for example in *Lysis,* in the question: In that which is dear (*philon*) to us, what ultimately is the dear as such? If we continue to ask for the sake of what, we shall run out of breath unless we can arrive at a beginning which no longer refers to other dear things, but in which our questioning comes to rest in that which is basically dear, for the sake of which we have declared all other things to be dear. Our endeavor is not directed toward the means that help us to attain the end, but toward the end itself, for the sake of which all these means are provided.

Or let us suppose, with *Charmides,* that there is a miraculous man who knows the whole past, present, and future, in short, a man from whom nothing is hidden. Which of all the branches of knowledge makes him happy, or do all do so equally: the art of playing drafts, arithmetic, medicine? It turns out that none of them, that no specialized science nor all together, enables men to live happily. A happy life is made possible only by the one knowledge, *knowledge of the good*. If this one knowledge is lacking, there can be no true benefit from any specialized knowledge. And this one knowledge is not prudence, nor is it the knowledge of knowledge and ignorance, but solely the knowledge of good and evil.

In *Euthydemus* knowledge and skill are distinguished from their purpose. He who makes the lyre does not make the music. The hunter provides food for the kitchen. The general hands his conquest over to the statesman. We require a knowledge and a skill (*technē*) that know how to utilize what they have gained possession of. Or to put it in another way: We require a knowledge and a skill, in which the activity that produces coincides with an understanding of how to use what has been produced. Even a skill that succeeded in making us immortal would be useless to us unless we knew how to make proper use of immortality. If we acquire knowledge and skill that do not coincide with a knowledge of how to use them, we are in the foolish position of children trying to catch larks: with each new science we think we have knowledge in our grasp, but each time it eludes us.

In this thinking we always sense a striving toward the goal where all searching ceases. Thus, in a certain indefinable sense, this thinking is always at the goal, but in regard to the definable, its positions are always changing. The ultimate answer is never given. The mere understanding can find no way out, and this perplexity determines the character of the early dialogues; essentially, it runs through all of Plato. Platonic philosophy begins with the Socratic thinking about *aretē* and keeps its tie with it to the end (*Discourse on the Good*). This mode of knowledge is amplified in the course of Plato's work and extended to the whole realm of knowledge: man, the state, the world. What is already present in the early dialogues runs through the whole of Plato's philosophizing, whose power of growth seems to know no limits.

Amid the quicksands of Sophism, Socrates, and with him Plato, strove to find solid ground in thinking itself. This becomes possible only through a new dimension of knowledge.

B. *The significance of this thinking:* The prevailing concept of knowledge, then as now, implies a knowledge of something. It always involves an object. I know it or I do not know it. If I acquire knowledge, I have a possession. I acquire it by an effort of my understanding and my memory. I can hand it on in the form of a skill. In application, this knowledge represents a power. I can make use of what I know; knowledge gives me a limited power over something else. This something else can be outside me or within me. It is not myself.

Plato considers this knowledge and uses it. He saves it from the intellectual confusion in which the meaning of all concepts is forever shifting, so that one can speak of nothing as permanent and identical, and everything becomes arbitrary. He looks for concepts that have a fixed, definable meaning, that are universal over against the many particular cases, and valid for all.

But this does not suffice. Plato's achievement has been seen in his founding of a cogent and demonstrable scientific knowledge. Perhaps he was the founder of scientific knowledge, but for him such knowledge is only a part of the prevailing concept of knowledge. The essential is elsewhere. The prevailing knowledge turned out to be a knowledge without aim or purpose, because it has no ultimate goal. It is a limited knowledge, because it binds us to particular things. It is not true knowledge, because it distracts us from the essential; and it is not fundamental, because it is not rooted in the source.

The ultimate goal would be achieved only if beyond all definite things we could attain to an absolute, if beyond all definable ends—which once again call forth the question "What for?"—we might attain to the self-sufficient, ultimate purpose, and beyond all particular goods, to the good itself. When he seeks sharp definitions of universal concepts, Plato is not interested in relatively sound definitions of this and that; but by using their language to probe the idea of the absolute, beyond which no further advance or question is possible, he is seeking a language of the absolute itself. That is why all finite definitions end in impasse, perplexity But in these perplexities the direction of the goal is sensed all the more acutely, though our ignorance of what it is becomes increasingly evident.

Measured by a knowledge which provides meaning and measure and decision in outward and inner action, the prevailing knowledge which supposes it *has* the thing it knows, is congealed, incomplete, and unjustifiably complacent. It can acquire its truth only by bursting its limits, by understanding itself in the knowledge of nonknowledge.

Fundamental knowledge is not, like the prevailing knowledge, a knowing of something; it is one with the reality of the knower. Through the richest unfolding of the knowledge of something, fundamental knowledge finds itself in a realm where it need no longer know any something; this is the realm of knowledge, where knowledge is at home.

As long as Plato is thus trying to attain fundamental knowledge through demonstrable knowledge, he can provide no doctrine akin to the doctrines prevailing in branches of knowledge that deal with something, concerning the content of fundamental knowledge. This knowledge cannot be communicated as a dogmatic finding; it cannot be developed into a system. But what does become possible is an orderly speaking in questions and answers (investigation) in the hope of finding a path (method) upon which the final illumination provides guidance without becoming an object. To live knowingly is man's supreme possibility. The injunction to lead the right life coincides with the claim of such thinking.

What makes this knowledge that is always in motion so hard to grasp is that the thinking it demands is something more than the object thinking implied in the prevailing concept of knowledge. It takes up definite, logically formulable contents of knowledge and operates with them to pass beyond them. This path seems to attain both at once—it demonstrates and deduces cogent object knowledge and at the same time opens up access to the eternally actual origin. Such thinking is impenetrable to the mere understanding, which grasps only the immediately demonstrated contents, and if left to itself, without background and guidance, moves endlessly and aimlessly from fact to fact.

Platonic thinking is not based on the invention of a method, a technique that can be applied and repeated at will, by which, as in scientific investigation, new results are achieved by the collaboration of many. It is a process which went on throughout Plato's life, taking on ever new forms, endlessly inventive, but making no definite progress. In the clarity of thinking it seeks to reveal what is not yet encompassed in this clarity. The end cannot be attained in human existence, but what is revealed in this striving for fundamental knowledge exerts an immense attractive force.

Plato became aware of the power and limits of thinking. If truth is to become real, each thought in its objective fixations must be transcended; then it will not, in the form of rational certainty, become a false ground of existence; it will not become a lazy man's bed for us who search but should not possess, or an evasion for us who should go onward, or a hiding place for delusions. This is what Goethe meant when he said that Plato "dispels all objects with his method."

c. *The essential characteristics of this thinking:*

1. *It is directed toward the One: Aretē* is one, not many. The highest authority is one. When the theory of Ideas was developed, the One was called the Idea of the good. But neither in the form of *aretē,* nor of the highest authority, nor of the good, is this One a universal concept under which all phenomena are subsumed as cases. It is not the goal for which we strive. It is not a standard by which we distinguish correct and incorrect. No, it is what truly illumines all definite concepts, what grounds all aims in an absolute aim beyond which we can question no further, what first makes the merely correct true. It is the guiding principle; to think and live toward it lends meaning to existence.

We cannot know this One exactly as we know definite concepts. But we find no satisfaction in what we know without it, even with the utmost precision. In all our thinking, in our exact thinking which indefatigably— and rightly so—strives for a maximum of precision, we are oriented toward what we do not know exactly, what we cannot know with the definite knowledge of the understanding, namely the ineffable One, which guides us while remaining open, which, though touched upon in the clearest discourse, can be experienced only in the illumination that transcends the understanding and all palpable intelligibles.

2. *It is one with self-awareness:* Anyone who reflects knows that he does so. Reflection and self-knowledge are one. Reflection alone is a knowledge of other knowledge and of itself. No existent has a natural relation to itself, but can only be related to something else. The only exception is thinking which is conscious of itself.

Self-awareness seeks to be one with itself. "I would rather that my lyre should be inharmonious . . . or that the whole world should be at odds with me, and oppose me, rather than that I, being one, should be at odds with myself, and contradict myself."

Only one who is consistent with himself can agree with others. To achieve harmony in oneself is to make friends with oneself and gain others as friends.

Thus being oneself is the characteristic (*oikeion*) of man, his fundamental and authentic quality. What is best for each man is what is most his own; but this can only reside in the good. "Men are quite willing to have their feet or their hands amputated if they believe those parts of themselves to be diseased; for people are not attached to what particularly belongs to them, except in so far as they can identify what is good with what is their own, and what is bad with what is not their own."

3. The new thinking is not essentially an acquisition of something other, but a soaring of one's own being: with this knowledge man is transformed. A transcending of one's own nature through thinking, guided by whatever is revealed in thought, is the basic trait of philosophical reflection from Plato down to Kant's formulation of enlightenment as "man's exodus from a state of tutelage for which he himself has been to blame."

Therefore no knowledge is indifferent. Even in its seemingly most irrelevant forms, it may well become a factor of transcendence. No knowledge is without its effect on the soul. Knowledge is not like a foodstuff. You can take a foodstuff home in a bag and, if you wish, ask an expert whether it is fit to eat. But you cannot put knowledge into a container; you can take it home only by incorporating it in your mind, and you have no way of knowing whether you have done yourself good or harm in the process. From philosophical thinking arises the conscience that makes me responsible for what I allow to enter into myself, for what I concern myself with. What I read, hear, see, what work I do, the possibilities of knowledge and feeling that I encourage, how I choose and how I keep my distance—none of all this is indifferent; everything takes on reality in what I am and become.

D. *Two propositions that follow from the Idea of fundamental knowledge:* Only in view of this Platonic concept of knowledge in contradistinction to the current one, can we understand and recognize the truth of the following two strange judgments.

1. *"Ignorance is the greatest evil."* The accursed murderer of Dion is indeed accused of lawlessness and godlessness, but above all he is accused of "presumptuous ignorance, that root of all evil among men." If ignorance is mere folly, it leads only to childish misdemeanors; it is only weakness. But if ignorance is combined with a false claim to knowledge and with power to boot, it becomes the source of the gravest crimes. Presumption in knowledge is the worst of evils. It is ignorance to suppose you have knowledge itself in the knowledge you can acquire by learning, to suppose that knowledge resides in the endless inventory of knowable things. Knowledge is knowledge in nonknowledge under the guidance of the good. A philosopher is one who strives for knowledge with all his being, but for the fundamental knowledge to which finite knowledge is a means. The acquisition of finite, limited, and, as such, misleading knowledge has meaning and truth and is an indispensable path if it is guided by fundamental knowledge. This knowledge is one with its effect, which is always salutary. Where there is no effect, there is no knowledge. Where the effect is evil, the explanation lies in the ignorance of limited knowledge that makes false claims.

2. *"No one can do wrong voluntarily."* We say that men are overpowered

by rage and desire, that we perform an action although we know it to be harmful, that we want what we do not want. According to Plato, all this is impossible. For "the disagreement between pain and pleasure with respect to reasoned judgment is the worst ignorance; but it is also the greatest, because it affects the great mass of the soul." So speaks Plato in his last work, *The Laws,* where he once again repeats a sentence that occurs frequently beginning with the early dialogues: "No one can do wrong voluntarily." This proposition can have meaning only if we have in mind not finite but fundamental knowledge.

Finite knowledge is either indifferent, without consequences, or it has consequences in the technically governable world outside me and within me; it brings about no transformation in its possessor. Such knowledge does not seem to affect him; hence it is neutral in regard to good and evil, it can be used and misused. This knowledge is regarded "as a slave that lets itself be dragged about by all other states of mind." Only fundamental knowledge gives this finite knowledge guidance and so dispels its neutrality. In the fundamental knowledge of justice I myself become just. It is no longer a knowledge that can exist in itself, without consequences. But the consequences are knowledge itself. Knowledge and the application of knowledge are no longer distinguishable. If a man knows what is right and does the opposite, it means that he did not truly know.

This brings us to the relation between will and knowledge: The true will is the knowing will. The desire that overpowers is not will but ignorance. Only he wills—and is not merely driven—who wills the good. Only he who does what is right acts freely. In fundamental knowledge, the good and the right are one with the will. Here one can no longer speak of passions controlled by will. Where there is true knowledge, which is at the same time true will, what is incompatible with it ceases to be. Because it no longer is, it does not have to be combated.

The proposition that no one can voluntarily do wrong, that one cannot knowingly, contrary to one's knowledge, commit an evil act, applies only to genuine knowledge. With finite knowledge, which as such remains ignorance, I can act intentionally with a view to satisfying my lust, anger, violence, or I can act unintentionally from mere passion. In finite knowledge of something, I can also do something harmful against my better knowledge; I can either take evil consequences into account or put them out of mind. For this knowledge, which is a knowledge of something, is not the knowledge that is identical with the reality of the thinking man. As such it partakes of the ignorance that is the greatest of evils.

It might seem as though all finite reality vanished in this Platonic thinking with its aspiration to what is highest. Two questions become urgent: (1) Can such thinking be communicated, and if so, how? Plato considers this question explicitly. The answer is provided in the dialogue form, his use of irony and playfulness, his dialectic method. (2) What is the substance of this thinking, or its motive force, or the fulfillment that is already present in the search? The answer is the Platonic Eros.

2. *The Question of Communicability*

As we have seen, knowledge is divided into the usual knowledge, which possesses and disposes of something, and fundamental knowledge, which first gives meaning to this ordinary knowledge. The two are not communicable in the same way. The contents of mathematical, astronomical, medical knowledge, or of craftsmanship, can be taught simply and directly. But what of the truth that is in them, the truth of their correctness, the source and goal from which this teachable knowledge and all life derive their meaning, the knowledge whose measure is not man but which is the measure of man? How can it be communicated and taught?

The truth in knowledge, which admits of the expressible, definable object as a medium but not as the ultimate form of knowledge—can this truth be framed in speech? Having no object, does it not seep away into the ineffable? But a truth that cannot be communicated in any way is no longer truth. If direct communication is impossible, we must communicate indirectly. How this can be done became with Plato a fundamental question of philosophy. He did not answer it conclusively. It can neither be understood nor solved by purely theoretical insight. Plato was first to see the radical importance of this question.

In the *Seventh Letter* he speaks directly of the communication of truth: "With it, it is not the same as with other things we learn: it cannot be framed in words, but from protracted concentration devoted to the object and from spending one's life with it, a light suddenly bursts forth in the soul as though kindled by a flying spark, and then it feeds on itself." The unsaid and unsayable is communicated indirectly in speech, but only in the speech without reservation that takes place in the encompassing community. In the inspiration of the moment it flares up among men, but only among men joined in an enduring bond.

For this reason Plato thought little of written communication and says in his *Seventh Letter:* "Concerning the essentials I have written no book nor shall I write one." Plato is far from saying that he is keeping secret something that can be said. He means that by its very nature the essential refuses to be fixated in doctrine, for in such fixation it would be lost.

Yet, in apparent contradiction to this view, Plato created a written work which for depth and greatness has no equal in all the history of philosophy. He wrote with extreme care and admirable self-discipline. There is no doubt that he attached great importance to his writings. And yet in his own judgment this lifework consisted merely of intimations and reminiscences; it was not a communication of the essence. But then it becomes important for us to ask: What did Plato actually attempt to do in his written work? How was he able to achieve a maximum of true communication?

A. *The dialogue:* It cannot be an accident that nearly all Plato's works are in dialogue form. Form and substance are concomitant. It is impossible to suppose that the philosophy was there first and that then Plato chose the dialogue as the best possible way of communicating it. If this philosophizing was to be communicated in writing, the dialogue form was its necessary expression. When Plato's philosophy is expounded undialectically as a doctrine, it becomes scarcely recognizable.

The Platonic dialogues show a great diversity of form. There is no standard pattern, and it is hard to find two that are formally quite alike (perhaps *Sophist* and *Statesman,* or *Timaeus* and *Laws*). It is important for the reader to feel this diversity. Taken as a whole, the dialogues transport us into a world long past, a world of extraordinary men who speak with all their intellectual spontaneity. We see the aristocratic society of Athens, its freedom, urbanity, malice. We experience many moods, earnestness amid merriment, a conviviality from which all heaviness and narrowness have vanished. We witness scenes on the street, in the *gymnasion*, at banquets, in the country, in the court of justice. We attend the conversation of statesmen, simple citizens, poets, physicians, Sophists and philosophers, boys and young men.

Amid this teeming life, philosophical discussions are recorded. Some of the dialogues seem to be reports of discussions at the Academy. Even when they suggest translations of lectures into dialogue form, they preserve their atmosphere of ease—one is never conscious of any effort—and at the same time the free spirit that cannot be captured in concepts and formulas and dogmas but moves freely and masterfully among them.

Such portrayal is comparable to literary creation. The great novelists of the modern era (above all Dostoevski and Balzac) also depict a world in which philosophical discussions are frequent. Like them, Plato seems to portray the whole gamut of possibility, to give each character his due, to remain impartial, to show what is, and without judging as to good and evil, to leave each man his existence in the light of good and evil at once. But the great difference is that the substance of Plato's work is not the portrayal of a world, but the philosophical truth that lies in thinking. Since this thinking cannot be adequately communicated in formal lectures, it invites all means of exploration—even the writing of dialogues—but never surrenders itself or its claim to pre-eminence. Plato dissociates himself from the poet. Poets, he says, are not quite right in their mind. In representing persons of conflicting opinion, they are often at odds with themselves, not knowing whether the one opinion or the other is true. In Plato's intention, his poetic dialogue is always guided by a single reference point, the one and eternal truth, which can call attention to itself only indirectly through the whole texture of discussion, teaching, verification, argumentation, confutation.

Plato needs poetic invention in order to represent the truth in which didactic exposition is only a factor. As with the novelist or narrative poet, it is impossible to know with rational certainty which position is Plato's, which of the speakers represents his view: Plato portrays thinking men; he lets his figures speak; he himself does not speak. It is an oversimplification to say with Diogenes Laertius that Socrates, the stranger from Elea, Timaeus, the Athenian host, are the characters in the dialogues who say what Plato regards as right. Like a poet, Plato raises ideas to their full potentiality. This permits him to hold his own position in suspense. However, we cannot understand his philosophical dialogue with an attitude of aesthetic neutrality; it demands of the reader an experience of serious self-realization, and only such an experience can enable us to understand it. For the dialogue is an indirect communication of truth through the forms of philosophical thought.

The one goal remains this thinking of the truth. The first step is always liberation from the rigidity of rationally determined but sharply developed finite positions, hence a skepticism in the usual sense of the word, whose purpose it is, however, to make use of the fully developed understanding as a means of receiving absolute truth, meaning, and guidance from a higher source. In his own reflection on dialogue, Plato makes several points that have a bearing on all human truth:

The individual finds no truth. To achieve certainty in his thinking, he needs another, with whom he can speak. The conversation must always be between two, not among several at once. The others listen until the conversation comes around to the points where it will be advanced by the right interruptions or disturbed by the wrong ones. The value of a statement lies in its own intellectual position, not in the approval of those present. "For in regard to the value of what I say, I can call on only one witness, my adversary with whom I am carrying on the discussion; as to the crowd, I ignore it; I can obtain the consent of only one man, it is not with the crowd that I am speaking." Dialogue is a continuous growth of certainty; your opponent agrees, contradicts, follows you, and in all this the question remains open: "For what I say I do not say as one who knows; rather, I join you in searching."

Dialogue is the *reality of thinking itself.* Speaking and thinking are one. What is thinking? "A discourse that the mind carries on with itself about any subject it is considering . . . when the mind is thinking, it is simply talking to itself, asking questions and answering them, and saying, Yes or No. So I should describe thinking as a discourse, and judgment as a statement pronounced, not aloud to someone else, but silently to oneself."

Dialogue is the *way to the truth.* An enemy of the truth who accepts dialogue is lost. An attitude of fundamental hostility to the truth and hence to communication makes dialogue an absurdity. For this reason dogmatists and nihilists reject any true dialogue. They rob dialogue of its nature. All governments that desire untruth reject discussion with the adversary or, if they have the power, forbid it.

With Socrates, Plato consciously brought philosophy into a situation of question and answer, and going further, of dialogue in all its potentialities. Let the philosopher give an account of his thinking in every kind of communication with other men—a communication in which logical arguments play an important but not the ultimate part; in which they are indispensable but not decisive.

Plato reflects on the different kinds of philosophical discussion which at the same time he records. He represents long speeches, swift exchanges, disagreement; he shows men talking at cross purposes and then seeking the simplest and most direct understanding in concise dialogue; he shows men failing to understand one another. In short, he shows what it means for men to speak together.

He stresses the difference between *long speeches* and the discussion advancing in short sentences, between harangues to the people and real discussion (*Protagoras, Gorgias, Republic*). Long speeches have their drawbacks: one forgets what has been said; one evades the question in point. Dialogue on the other hand makes it possible to attain agreement step by step, to arrive at logically compelling conclusions in the precision of question and answer, in the battle of alternatives. Thus the speaker, instead of letting himself be judged by his listeners, is at once speaker and judge, so that true agreement is attained. Socrates asks his partners to accept this method, and lets them decide who should ask the questions; the guidance must always be in the hands of one contestant, but the roles can be exchanged. When one participant protests indignantly that in free Athens he should be entitled to speak as long as he pleases, Socrates replies yes, but that he in turn is free not to listen. Protagoras says: If I had done what you demand, I should never have bested anyone in an argument and should have no name among the Greeks.

With their innumerable portraits of men speaking together, of successful and unsuccessful discussion, with their explanation of the conditions of success, Plato's dialogues became for all time a model and a guide for all men who wish really to speak together.

The first requirement for dialogue is *ability to listen*. One who wishes to speak with other men must remain open to persuasion and not suppose himself to be in ultimate possession of the truth. In answer to Philebus' "I say, and I shall always say," Socrates remonstrates: "Surely we are not now simply contending in order that my view or yours may prevail. I presume that we ought both of us to be fighting for the truth."

The mere *polemic discourse* which serves no other purpose than to annihilate the enemy is a very different matter from the discourse aimed at communication with a view to the truth. Plato portrays the methods of intellectual homicide in ostensible discussion. The speaker aims for effect, tries to gain the advantage by an impressive conclusion, does what he can to get the laugh on his side. Discourse has become a mere weapon; what is in essence a medium of understanding has become a means of mutual deception. Plato discloses the logical stratagems (eristics), which were later systematized by Aristotle.

True conversation also requires *good manners*. It requires candor and an attitude of benevolence toward the other. Not only the logical forms, but an understanding of their place in conversation is prerequisite to the discovery of truth in dialogue. Socrates is a picture of urbanity, of freedom from malice even in the most impassioned debate, of communication cloaked in questions, and of the possibilities of playfulness. Bad manners in discussion include: speaking as though handing out orders; refusal to stick to the subject; wanting to be right at all costs; breaking off the discussion with a "What you say is of no interest to me" or an "I simply don't understand you."

True dialogue requires us to see our opposite at his best. "The best thing, if it were possible, would be to make our adversaries better: but if this is impossible, let us try in our conversation to make them seem to have improved, by proceeding on the assumption that they are willing to answer in more orderly fashion and more to the point than is now the case."

Since it is necessary to *understand the matter under discussion* in order to understand the dialogue, a picture of the general trend can be formed only by a reader who takes an interest in these matters. If we limit ourselves to what seems to be understandable even without this understanding of the subject, to the portrayal of persons and situations, the tone of the speaking, we shall not even understand these, or we shall take an aesthetic view of them that can only mislead us.

But an understanding of the themes is not enough. Though dialogue is a vessel for the thinking of oppositions, we are not dealing with simple logical antithesis apportioned between two persons, but with men who meet in their thinking and therein disclose themselves. In dialogue we discern tendencies which provoke and complement one another. Since the manner of thinking can communicate itself only in thought contents, the content itself is dramatized in dialogue. The crucial turns of thought become dramatic climaxes.

In the greatest of the dialogues, Plato has succeeded inimitably in relating scene, situation, and characters to the ideas brought forward. The thought content itself takes on visible form. Love (Eros), the theme of *Symposium,* takes on reality in each of the participants and in Socrates achieves its full reality. In *Phaedo* the dying Socrates discusses immortality with the grief-stricken young men. Nonbeing, the topic of *Sophist,* is represented in the person of the Sophist, who is himself a nonentity. The thought content is illustrated by the actions and attitudes of the speaker or his opponent. Thus the dialogue form, through the relation of the content to men and situations, makes it possible to actualize the existential meaning of ideas along with their logical meaning.

Eristic speeches, the tricks which seem to crush the adversary by logic, are possible only because of the contradictions in thought itself. Plato's dialogue shows the fundamental truth of the contradictory movement of ideas. Not obstinate insistence on one's assertions, but only the art of mastering contradictions helps to combat truthless eristics. The danger is implicit in the nature of discourse and can only be combated by knowledge of it. A man unskilled in the understanding of discourse (*logoi*) may first be full of confidence in a speech and regard it as true; a little later he may, sometimes rightly, sometimes wrongly, decide that it is false. In the end, particularly where polemics are concerned, he may conclude that he has gained great wisdom in the insight that there is no truth in anything or in any discourse, but rather that everything keeps twisting and turning, so that there is nowhere any stability or certainty. This leads to misology, just as the disillusionment of those who do not learn how to deal with men leads to misanthropy.

The *demonstration of contradictions* has two essential consequences for all philosophizing.

1. As an "art of purification," it opens the way to knowledge by showing men what they do not know. People who think they know refuse to learn. But when a man who prattles on, confident in the soundness of his judgments, is subjected to questioning, here is what happens: he replies first one way and then another. By juxtaposing his contradictions, the dialectic art proves that his changing opinions "referring at one and the same time to the same object are in contradiction with each other." He is taught to know only what he really knows. For with all this pointing out of contradictions, "the truth is never confuted." Openness to correction is acquired by education and is a sign of distinction, whereas the man who is inaccessible to correction, be he the king of kings, must be regarded as an uncultivated man, whose mind has suffered hideous neglect.

2. The demonstration of contradictions brings thinking into its natural *movement.* Its consequence in the dialogue form is that the thought content is suspended in the movement of thinking. While in an exposition thoughts are set forth as definitive, in dialogue the truth develops spontaneously, in the course of the exchange, as an objective reality that is not contained in any one position. It is not as though a truth that might be expressed directly and more adequately in an exposition were superfluously cloaked in dialogue form. For in dialogue my opponent also makes an indispensable contribution to the truth in its entirety.

B. *Irony and playfulness:* If Socratic irony could be replaced by direct communication, there would be no need for it. A proper understanding of the indirect meaning of irony requires not only practice in rational thinking but also training in philosophical sensibility. This irony is varied and complex. The intermingling of truth and falsehood, the ambiguity that can become truth only for those who hold the key to it, must lead to constant misunderstanding. Plato seems to say: Let those who cannot understand misunderstand. Sometimes there seems to be anger beneath the frothy surface. In this communication where rationality ceases, understanding cannot be forced by rational arguments. In profound irony there is concern for the genuine truth. It deters us from supposing that we possess the truth in object knowledge, in the work, in the figure, which, magnificent as they may be, become untrue the moment we take them as absolutes.

An ambiguous irony can quickly lose its profound meaning. Without meaning of its own, it becomes an instrument of destruction, the language of nihilism. Laughter kills. This irony follows the principle of Gorgias: answer the ridiculous with seriousness, the serious with ridicule. This irony discloses nothing but nothingness. It is not the self-effacing language of the Eros, but a weapon serving the power of nothingness. Directed against all seriousness as such, it is the groundless warfare of a tumultuous nonbeing.

Philosophical irony, on the other hand, expresses the certainty of a fundamental meaning. Perplexed by the discrepancy between the simplicity of rational discourse and the ambivalence of appearances, it strives to attain the truth, not by saying it but by awakening it. It strives to give an intimation of the hidden truth, whereas nihilistic irony is empty. In the whirl of appearances, philosophical irony strives to lead, by true disclosure, to the ineffable presence of the truth, whereas empty irony leads from the whirl of appearances to nothingness. Philosophical irony is a diffident fear of directness, a safeguard against the direct misunderstanding that is total.

All this is to be found in Plato's dialogues. Here we find irony on three levels. First there is the obvious irony, the direct falsehood with which Socrates leads his opponent up a false track, or graciously spares his feelings, or delivers a cutting attack. On the next level we find the attitude of fundamental irony by which Socrates seeks to provoke the knowledge of nonknowledge. At the highest level, Plato creates a general atmosphere of betweenness; this irony resides in the absolute ambiguity of all finite, determinate things. It is only in this ambiguity, this total irony where everything loses its fixity, that the heart of being discloses itself. Ideas and myths are like arrows shot off toward the realm where even the name of being must vanish. Discursive philosophy merely explores possibilities along the way. It is earnest—not with the dark earnestness of the dogmatic possessor of the truth or the angry earnestness of nihilistic mockery, but with the earnestness of freedom (*eleutheriotēs*), which can perfectly well be playful. Two examples may give an idea of this total irony in which Plato includes himself:

Speaking of literature, he ironically disparages his own activity as a philosophical writer. His own literary works, he declares, are not the seed, which is what he takes seriously, but mere bowers of Adonis (baskets of flowers for the festival of Adonis), planted in play and quick to fade; while others distract themselves with other pleasures, he amuses himself for a moment watching his plants sprout. There is always an element of play in the written word, he says, and never was a word written or spoken, in poetry or prose, that deserved to be taken quite seriously.

All men's occupations are viewed in an ambiguous light. "Human affairs are hardly worth considering in earnest, and yet we must be in earnest about them," though there is no great happiness to be derived from it. Only the serious deserves to be taken seriously. That is God. Man is God's artfully constructed toy, and that is the most a man can aspire to be. Consequently, men and women should do nothing but play the best possible games. For the most part we are mere puppets in the hands of the gods, with only the barest fragment of truth and reality. When, having spoken these words, he was accused of holding the human race in very low esteem, he replied: "Forgive me:—I was comparing them with the gods, and under that feeling I spoke." In this light, mankind is deserving of a certain respect. Thus in the irony of his disillusionment with men, men are puppets only in comparison with the gods. And this irony has its limits: an area is left open for man.

3. *Idea, Dialectic, Eros*

A THE "THEORY OF IDEAS"

A. *The highest authority, the* agathon: From the very outset Plato searched for the supreme authority, knowledge of which first lends meaning to all thought and action. He calls it the highest science (*megiston mathēma*). To attain it, no effort is too great. It is the only important thing. Its object is the good (*agathon*). A Platonic parable gives an idea of what the good is: The good in the realm of thought is like the sun in the realm of the visible. We do not see the sun, but we see everything in its light. What in the realm of the visible the sun is to the eye (the most sunlike of all the organs of sense perception) and to what is seen, the good, in the realm of the thinkable, is to reason (man's highest faculty) and to what is thought. If the mind is undeviatingly directed toward that which is illumined by the light of the good or of true being, it knows and seems to be in possession of reason. But when it looks upon what is mixed with darkness, on things that come into being and pass away, it becomes dull-sighted and falls a prey to mere opinion, devoid of all reason.

Just as vision is sunlike but not the sun itself, so true knowledge is related to the good, but is not the good itself. Just as the sun not only lends things the faculty of being seen, but gives them change, growth, and nourishment, though itself free from change, so the good gives to the knowable not only the power to be known, but also being and essence, though itself not a being. For in dignity and power, it towers even above being (*epekeina tēs ousias*).

B. *The world of Ideas. Two worlds:* What is it then that has its eternal being from the good, from that which is above being? What is it that we think in the light of the good? It is a realm of Ideas of prototypes that stand unchanging above all change. It is the eternal realm of the essences: likeness and diversity as such, justice as such, beauty as such, bed and table as such, and so on for all the forms that we see before our eyes in their definite shapes.

To put it undialectically, there is a world of being (the realm of unchanging Ideas, without beginning and indestructible, neither receiving anything else into itself nor entering into anything else, itself hidden to the eye, an object of pure contemplation) and the world of becoming (changing, never resting, created, in continuous movement, arising in one place and there vanishing, apprehensible only by belief in bond with sense perception). But there is a third realm (*Timaeus*), space. Indestructible, it provides a place for all the things that come into being; in its eternal nonbeing, it is known without sense perception by a kind of inauthentic insight (bastard inference, *logismos nothos*). Space and the world of change within it are the realm to which we refer when we look about us as in a dream and say: Everything that exists must after all be in a definite place; what is neither on earth nor anywhere in the cosmos has no being. And because of the dream state we are in, we transpose these delusions to the realm of authentic, never slumbering being.

The realm of Ideas is called the supracelestial place (*hyperouranios topos*) or the place of intelligibles (*topos noētos*). It is adumbrated in metaphors and concepts: "There abides the very being . . . ; the colorless, formless, intangible essence, visible only to the mind, the pilot of the soul. . . . [There] she beholds justice, and temperance, and knowledge absolute, not in the form of generation, or of relation, which men call existence, but knowledge of absolute existence" (*Phaedrus*). The man whose soaring thought attains to its goal beholds "a beauty whose nature is marvelous indeed, the final goal of all his previous efforts. This beauty is first of all eternal; it neither comes into being nor passes away, neither waxes nor wanes; next, it is not beautiful in part and ugly in part, not beautiful at one time and ugly at another, nor beautiful in this relation and ugly in that, nor beautiful here and ugly there, as varying according to its beholders; nor again will this beauty appear to him like the beauty of a face or hands or anything else corporeal, or like the beauty of a thought or a science, or like beauty which has its seat in something other than itself, be it a living thing or the earth or the sky or anything else whatever; he will see it as absolute, existing alone with itself, unique, eternal."

One might be tempted to call such words empty, consisting only of negative statements and tautologies. But it is just this absence of all finite clarity that gives us an intimation of something that cannot be communicated in any other way. This is what gives Diotima's words their validity. "This above all others, she goes on to say, is the region where a man's life is worth living. . . . Do you think that it will be a poor life that a man leads who has his gaze fixed in that direction . . . and is in constant union with it? Do you not see that in that region alone . . . will he be able to bring forth not mere reflected images of virtue [*aretē*] but true virtue. . . . And having brought forth and nurtured true virtue, he will be beloved of God, and become, if ever a man can, immortal himself."

Thus Plato knows two worlds: the world of Ideas and that of the senses, the world of being and that of becoming, the noetic (intelligible) world and the world of appearance.

c. *The relation between the two worlds:* The fundamental form of this Platonic thinking is the cleavage (*tmēma*) between the changing world of temporal things and the eternal world of enduring things (and again between the world of Ideas and the realm beyond it, where the formulable knowledge that dwells in the world of Ideas soars to ineffable contact with the One and the good). From this fundamental separation (*chōrismos*), this cleavage that runs through being, the question follows: How are the two worlds related?

The things of the world of change are conceived as participating in the Ideas, and it is to this participation (*methexis*) that the things owe their being (situated between nonbeing and genuine being); or the other way around, the relation is seen as a presence (*parousia*) of the Ideas in the things. Or else the Idea is likened to an archetype or prototype (*paradeigma*), the thing to a copy or imitation (*mimēsis*).

d. *What is an Idea?* A list of the terms employed by Plato gives us a rather confusing picture. Some of them are: form (*eidos*), shape (*morphē*), type (*genos*), essence (*ousia*), unity (*monas, henas*); "what," "what it is," "self" (beauty itself, the horse itself), "as such"; "what is," "what beingly is" (*ontōs on*). Or he designates it by the singular instead of the plural: the horse in contradistinction to the horses; the beautiful in contradistinction to beautiful things; being in contradistinction to the things that are.

The question of what is included in the world of Ideas, of whether everything which in any way is also has its Idea, is discussed in the *Parmenides,* where he lists the Ideas of likeness of size (*isotēs*) and likeness of kind (*homoiotēs*), the Ideas of the just, the beautiful, of man and of other living creatures, of manufactured articles, table, bed, of the elements, fire, water, and even of mud, dirt, and other base things. In one passage, he speaks of five higher Ideas: being, likeness, otherness, rest, motion (*Sophist*).

The good, that which is beyond being, is also called an Idea. But the name is misleading. For the good is distinguished from all other Ideas. They are the static, inactive prototypes or models of the things that are, while it is the creative power that confers being itself.

E. *What is the reasoning behind the theory of Ideas?* A thought content as such is always timeless. The content of the Pythagorean theorem is timeless, its discovery and all subsequent thinking of its content are temporal. Through mathematical insight into compelling truths which are timeless, one discovers a being that is permanent and unchanging. We discover the universal, the true, which we cannot evade once we understand it, and in it we experience a perfect certainty.

The concept whereby a thing has unity and is what it is, is enduring: the individual horse perishes but the concept of the horse endures.

We do not derive what we recognize as enduring from sense perception, but we discover it with the help of sense perception: the mathematician makes use of visible forms; the object of his thinking, however, is not these forms but those of which they are the copies: the square as such, the diagonal as such. The figures serve as illustrations which merely help us learn what can be known only through the understanding (*dianoia*).

To our sensory perception of the continuously changing world we add a knowledge that is timeless and enduring. We had this knowledge before our perception (later it came to be termed *a priori* knowledge in contradistinction to *a posteriori* experience). In the *Meno*, Plato shows (by the example of mathematics) how in thinking we learn, as though merely recollecting it, what we actually knew before. In philosophizing, we think we see things as metaphors. "Time is the moving image of eternity." All images belong to time and space; the true being that appears to us through the images is timeless and spaceless.

F. *The dogmatic interpretation of the theory of Ideas:* In view of the manifold meanings embodied in the theory of Ideas, any attempt to reduce it to a principle and interpret it as a whole is futile. There is no unified theory of Ideas, but only a complex of notions, some of which run through the whole work from the earliest dialogues, while others make their appearance later. The Ideas play an essential role in the ascent of thought toward true being, but their expression changes according to the manner in which the search is communicated. When they become fixated in a doctrine which creates insoluble problems, Plato himself takes a critical view of them. He asks questions: Are there Ideas only of the good, or also of the bad? How are all the many Ideas related to one another? How can they be and at the same time not be? The Ideas are not only prototypes, species, unities. Ultimately the forms of all existents become numbers (not as quantities, but as individual primal forms). They are articulated in different ways. In some of the later dialogues they are not even mentioned, and in one of the last (*Timaeus*) they reappear in their simplest form, namely as the models that the Demiurge contemplates while fashioning the world. A line seems to run from the perplexities (particularly in the early dialogues) to the theory of Ideas and thence to the ineffable. The frame seems to grow steadily wider, the place of action more open and at the same time more richly inhabited; as to the solution, it is never complete.

Historically, the theory of Ideas lived on in an attractive but inadequate simplification. What remained of it was the realm of eternal essences or archetypes—the notion of the eternal truths revealed in the visions of poets and artists and in the meditations of the philosophers. In the triad of the good, the beautiful, the true (*agathon, kalon, sophon*), first uttered by Plato, it passed into a familiar phrase.

G. *The parable of the cave:* The theory of Ideas is brought home to us most forcefully in the celebrated parable of the cave (*Republic,* Book VII), illustrating our human situation and the knowledge and action that are possible in it.

Men live in an underground cave, their legs and necks chained so they cannot move. They can only see straight ahead, for the chains prevent them from turning their heads. Above and behind them a fire is blazing at a distance, and between the fire and the prisoners there is a raised path, beside which runs a low wall. Along the wall men pass carrying all manner of statues and figures. Some of them are talking, others are silent. Of all these things and of each other the prisoners see only the shadows cast by the fire on the wall opposite from them. They take the shadows of the objects for the truth and imagine that the words they hear are spoken by the passing shadows.

And now a wonderful thing happens. The prisoners are unchained. When one of them is compelled to stand up and turn his neck, he suffers sharp pains. His eyes are blinded by the glare of the fire. He is unable to recognize the things whose shadows he saw before. He believes that the shadows were more real and true than what is shown him now. If he were compelled to look at the fire, his eyes would hurt. He would turn away and take refuge in the things to which he is accustomed. And these would indeed seem clearer to him.

But he is left no peace. He is dragged up the steep slope issuing from the cave. He comes out into the sunlight. But he feels only pain, he is dazzled, and he cannot distinguish anything at all in the light of the sun. He must grow used to it gradually. Then he sees the things of the outer world in this order: first and most easily the shadows, then reflections in the water, then real objects themselves, then at night the heavenly bodies, the light of the moon and stars, and finally by day the sunlight and the sun itself. Now he sees not mere reflections but all things in their full reality. He proceeds to reason that it is the sun which gives us the seasons, that it rules over all and is even in a certain sense the source of all the things he has seen in the cave. And now he considers himself fortunate, when he remembers his former abode. There honors and distinctions were conferred on those who most clearly perceived the shadows of the passing objects, who best remembered them, and were thereby best enabled to predict what would happen in the future. But now he would rather do anything than be enslaved to such false notions and live in such a way.

Now he returns to the cave to set the others free. At first his eyes, full of darkness, see nothing. He would make himself ridiculous if he tried to compete with the prisoners in interpreting the shadows. They would say that his ascent was to blame, that it had ruined his eyesight, and that any such attempt to rise was folly. And if he attempted to unchain them and lead them upward, they would kill him.

That is Plato's parable. It is extraordinarily rich in implications. It can be taken as a metaphor for the two worlds and the modes of knowledge prevailing in them; for the ways of human life and the two kinds of blindness springing from opposite causes; for the modes of truth; and for transcendence as the essence of human being and human knowledge. Here there is no need to set forth these interpretations, either those presented by Plato himself or those that have been added. The parable with its interpretations is unforgettable. It is a miracle of philosophical invention, providing an approach to thoughts that do not lend themselves to direct statement.

Certain themes of the parable have lived on in history: the image of man as a cave dweller, the metaphysics of light which played so important a role in medieval philosophy, the sun as the author of all life. Moreover, the parable states three themes that play a determining role in all Platonic philosophizing: the turning around, the stages of knowledge, the twofold direction of human life.

H. *The turning around:* Human insight requires a turning around (*metastrophē, periagōgē*). It is not given from outside as though eyes had been set in one's head (they are already there) or a seed had been implanted. But as in the cave the turning of the eyes involves the whole body, so knowledge, in turning from the realm of becoming to the realm of being, must take the whole mind with it. Accordingly education (*paideia*) is the art of bringing about such a turn. Because of its divine origin, the faculty of rational insight is always present—latently. But it becomes beneficent only through the turning; otherwise it is harmful.

I. *The doctrine of stages:* Knowledge advances by stages. From sense perception it proceeds to pure thought (in mathematics)—from pure thought to the Idea (from mathematical knowledge to dialectic science)—from the Idea to the realm beyond being (from Ideas to the Idea of the good).

Or to put it another way: from sensory experience it advances to right opinion (*doxa alēthēs*). From the *doxa* it advances by way of the sciences to the higher stage where the Ideas shine in their pure light, and thence to contact with that whereby the Ideas are enabled to shine and exist.

According to the aspect in which they are presented, the stages may be stages of knowledge, stages in man's being as a whole, stages of the existent. A rise from one to the other is at once a deepening of knowledge— self-realization in purity of mind—and an attainment to the vision of the highest. Dwelling as we do in the earlier stages, we tend to speak as if the higher ones did not exist. But dialogue at the lower stages can take on truth only through the guidance of the higher ones. If this guidance is lacking, we are governed by appearance and the communication that changes from one minute to the next. We remain obstinate and perplexed, because we lack an inner bond with the only guide to truth.

In order to attain to the upper stages, we must keep them always in mind. In themselves the lower stages are confined to incomprehension and ignorance. The consequence of this is that one who transcends the indispensable lower stages to attain to the higher objects, and who accordingly ventures into the higher stage of knowledge corresponding to them, finds himself in a strange situation. For the man who is confined to the lower stage, "the man versed in confutation has an easy time of it and if he wishes can convince most listeners that anyone who expresses his ideas in speech, writing, or response, is a bungler. . . ." For at the lower stages of knowledge the truth must move in contradictions. "But the listeners often fail to suspect that what is being confuted is not really what the mind thinks but the intrinsic inadequacy of the lower stages of knowledge."

J. *Two necessary directions in human life:* Two directions are open to the thinking mind: It can move from the world of appearance out into the eternal world (*Phaedo*); and again from the eternal world it can look back at the world of appearance with a view to understanding it and shaping it (*Republic, Laws, Timaeus*). Plato's philosophizing moves in both directions, toward being and from being. Man is "here" in the world; he must look beyond the world in order, by touching on the essential, to become essential himself. But then he comes back to the world. After turning away from the world he comes back to the mathematical and mythical understanding of the cosmos (*Republic, Timaeus*); after turning to the eternal regions from the life of the polis he is duty-bound to reconsider political life (*Republic, Laws*). Plato does not rise to the higher regions in order to abandon the world; his transcending does not lead to solitary ecstasy, deification. Plato and Plotinus both cast off the heaviness of the world. But Plotinus contents himself with release from the world, while Plato's philosophizing takes up its task in the world. However, Plato is equal to his work in the world only because he is at home in the supracelestial realm that is the source of norms and guidance.

B. DIALECTIC

We have spoken of the Ideas and have cited parables. To stop here would be to pass over the core of Plato's philosophic endeavor. Mere statement is not enough, for at crucial points the inquiring mind runs into difficulties. Thus the cleavage (*chōrismos, tmēma*) between being and becoming leads us either to conclude that they are unrelated or to ask how the gap is bridged. The answers in turn lead to impossible conclusions. If everything that is has its Idea, the Idea loses its character of goodness, for then it must include also the ugly, the evil, and the false. But according to the theory, what has no Idea can have no being. Each Idea is said to be independent, yet the Ideas are interrelated. They limit one another or depend on one another. This raises the question of what Ideas have in common.

In order to solve these difficulties we must *think* philosophically. Such thinking is what Plato calls dialectic. But it is not as though we first ran into difficulties and then had recourse to dialectic; no, it is in the methodic operations of the dialectic that we first become aware of what is at stake in philosophy. Dialectic is the thought-dynamic of the thinker who transforms himself in rising to higher knowledge. Thus Plato calls it the supreme science. Dialectic and philosophy are the same, the one stressing the method, the other the content.

A. *What is Platonic dialectic?* There are many brief and simple statements of what dialectic is, though they approach it from different angles:

It is the touchstone by which to determine who, forgoing the use of his eyes and all other sensory perception, is capable of advancing, in bond with the truth, to being itself (*Republic*). Dialectic is directed toward being, toward the always identical (*Philebus*). All other knowledge and ability serves only to bring in the spoils, which should be given to the dialectician to make use of (*Euthydemus*). Dialectic is the keystone to the edifice of knowledge; here the limit of all knowledge is attained (*Republic*). The knowledge of the dialectician is the mastery of all other knowledge (*Philebus*). Dialectic is the royal science (*basilikē epistēmē*) (*Euthydemus*); it is the knowledge of knowledge (*epistēmē epistēmōn*) (*Charmides.*)

In its rise to pure thought, in its apperception of being itself, dialectic transcends all provisional fixations, which without it would become dogmas. It opens up a free space where it moves in the play of ideas, and so, passing beyond the question of being, touches on the deep secret contained in it (particularly *Parmenides*). Dialectic is both thinking in its ascending movement and thinking in being itself; thus, it is either a dynamic that drives us forward or the eternal circular movement of speculation (particularly the second part of *Parmenides*).

B. *Illustrations of dialectic:* Let us try to clarify the essence of dialectic by examples of thought operations which Plato carries out and whose method he explains.

1. The movement of thought is kindled by oppositions: When we think of the world of sense perception, contradictions appear at once (as for example the paradoxes of motion). The contradictions clash like flint and steel and the spark they strike is the sought-for knowledge (*Republic*). "Serious things cannot be understood without laughable things, nor opposites at all without opposites" (*Laws*). To know the noble we must know the base. In action, to be sure, we must not follow the base, but we must know it if we are not to make ourselves ridiculous by sheer ignorance. Opposites are combined in all sensuous things, wherever there is space and time. But they are mutually exclusive. For no opposite can "ever be or become its own opposite, but either it passes away or perishes in the change."

But then Plato (in *Parmenides*) achieves the amazing insight that not only sensuous things, but the Ideas themselves contain contradictions.

In either case, in the world of things and the world of Ideas, what at first ends in perplexity becomes dialectically a means of speculation by which, with the contradictions themselves, one penetrates to deeper knowledge. Contradiction is the dynamic factor. It leads the eristic thinker through the decomposition of thought straight to nihilism. It "draws the dialectician toward Being" (*Republic*).

2. *Differentiation and synopsis:* Mere listing (the endless citing of examples) brings no insight into any question. The essence can be grasped only through an over-all vision (*synopsis*). In many individual cases the physician sees the recurrent form (*eidos*) of the sickness. To know a thing we must, by means of the logical understanding (*logismos*), gather its form (*eidos*), which is always one, from the many perceptions (*Phaedrus*). Plato is not yet thinking of the abstracting of a universal from many individual cases; what he has in mind is an apperception of unity of essence. "The chief test of a natural gift for dialectic . . . [is] the ability to see the connections of things" (*Republic*). But the truth of the over-all vision is always dependent on clarity of distinctions (*diairesis*). It is the differentiation that first gives thinking in oppositions its sharpness. Hence Plato's delight in distinctions, classifications, genus-species relations, in differentiation in all its forms, which "is a gift of the gods to men" (*Philebus*). It is this aptitude that leads the manifold to the unity of the type (in *synagōgē*). It defines the member of a class by bringing out the superordinate characteristics of the class and the particular differences. It leads to the reciprocal determination of ideas and thus to insight into what they have in common (their *koinōnia*), the one being a factor in the meaning of the others. The

structure of the world of Ideas is made clear and the thinker comes to feel at home in this realm of eternal form (*eidē*).

3. *The presuppositions and that which has no presupposition:* When the mathematician, guided by the visible figures, arrives, through the understanding (*dianoia*), at an exact determination of invisible relations, he always starts from presuppositions (such as the nature of a straight line, the different kind of figures, the three kinds of angles, etc.). He cannot go beyond these presuppositions. He regards them as self-evident.

But dialectic proceeds differently—by the hypothetic method. It tries out a hypothesis to see what follows from it, for example: If virtue can be taught, it must be knowledge (*Meno*). But then without images, working solely with concepts, dialectic thinks its way back to the beginning that precedes all presuppositions. Or rather, thinking (*logos*) attains to the beginning through dialectic; instead of taking the presuppositions as absolutely first and highest, it considers them as mere hypotheses, steps mounting to that which has no presupposition, the true beginning (*archē*) of the whole. Once it has apprehended the beginning, it descends again, retaining everything that is related to the beginning, but disregarding everything that can be perceived by the senses and working only with the concepts (*eidē*) and their inner relationships.

It is an indirect method. If man attempted to see being itself, he must fear to be blinded, as the eyes are blinded when they look into the sun. Thus it is necessary to operate by way of concepts (*logoi*) and to investigate the essence of things with their help. This is "the second best way." In this method, I start with a proposition (*logos*) that I regard as irrefutable. Then I assume that what seems compatible with it is true, and that what seems incompatible with it is untrue. For example, I start with the assumption: There is such a thing as the beautiful as such, the large as such, and so on. It follows that if something other than the beautiful as such is beautiful, this is so because it partakes of the beautiful as such. We disregard freshness of color, fine form, and so on—such qualities are mere sources of confusion— and simply state that "nothing else makes it beautiful than the presence (*parousia*) or participation (*koinōnia*) of the beautiful as such." We limit ourselves to the assertion that "all beautiful things become beautiful through the beautiful."

4. *The "between":* The dialectic of mere opposition remains aporetic and serves only as an indicator. Dialectic by intermediate concepts elucidates the divergent by establishing an intervening bond (*desmos*). Hence the importance of the "between" (*metaxy*), whereby separates are joined, whereby the one is present in the other or has a share in it. Hence also the importance of the moment (*exaiphnēs*), of the transition, the junction of past and future in the present. Hence also the being of what is not, which in a certain way has being.

Being and nonbeing are not ultimate opposites but are both present at every step, though in different ways: The *highest good* is beyond being, before being and nonbeing. The *world of Ideas* has being in every Idea, but in its divergence from another Idea, from otherness, every Idea is also non-being, which is expressed in the negative judgment "is not." The *world of becoming* is on the one hand being through participation in the Ideas, on the other hand nonbeing, insofar as it merely participates but does not fully "be." *Matter* or *space* is radically nonbeing, but with its potential becoming or coming-into-being, it is also an eternal potentiality toward being.

Plato describes (in *Sophist*) the "battle of giants" over being, between those on the one hand who regard all things as bodies in motion, who regard corporeity in space and time as identical with being and, on the other hand, those who regard only incorporeal, intelligible Ideas as truly real. The former are always left with something to which they cannot attribute corporeity: their insight, for example. The latter are driven into an untenable position. For: "Can we ever be made to believe that motion and life . . . have no place in perfect being? that it has neither life, nor thought, but stands immutable in solemn aloofness, devoid of intelligence?"

So it is with the One and the Other (*heteron*), or with the one and the many (*hen* and *polla*), also with the immutable and that which is "big and little," and also with the One and "the indefinite Two" (*aoristos dyas*), the limited and unlimited (*peras* and *apeiron*), or with the good and the many good things—in every case, we must search for the connection, the Encompassing wherein they unite, the intermediate links, the "between."

Let us try to sum up the substance of the dialectic:

Contradiction becomes a spur to motion, the medium in which opposites occur is being developed, and in both a "driving power toward being" is experienced. The objects of thought are ordered by differentiation and combination (*diairesis* and *synopsis*) in such a way that every meaning derives its definition from its place in the pyramid or family tree of concepts (in continuous dichotomic division); but all this is intended as an instrument of thinking toward being. Thinking on the basis of assumptions (*hypotheses*) and the question of the presuppositions of a statement strive to develop the connections between consequences, but with a view to rising above all presuppositions to that which has none. The thinking of opposites seeks the "between," in order, by clarifying the articulations, to penetrate to the ground whence they come or to the Encompassing that contains them all.

Of such dialectic, we may say: (1) The actual object of its search is not the universal relations it elaborates, for these are not self-sufficient, but instruments by which to rise higher. (2) According to Plato, it has even greater certainty and clarity (precision) than mathematics (for mathematics never achieves rational insight into its own premises). (3) For such dialectic, all arts, skills, sciences are mere prologues. The nonsensory nature of purely conceptual relations is held to cleanse the mind, preparing it for the journey to the suprasensory. For the thinking man the purpose of this activity is a turning around. But in this turning around the goal is not the man, but being itself, the One and immutable, which he can touch upon in thinking but not grasp.

Plato's dialectic was an answer to the dialectic that undermined all thought. Hence his insistence on the indispensable requirement for all dialectic: the definite concepts which enable us, when we use a word, to mean always the same thing. For we must form an identical view of things if we are to develop their consequences in a compelling way and achieve mastery over the limitless manifold. To arrive, by means of definite concepts, not at the eristic dialectic of disintegration (in which the concepts, instead of being set in a dialectic movement governed by method, are treated haphazardly), but at the dialectic of the speculative stage—that is Plato's method of thinking toward the truth.

c. *Objections to Plato's dialectic:* 1. It consists entirely of *analytic judgments,* which sometimes are presented with artless directness. For example: "The beautiful is beautiful only by virtue of the beautiful." Such thinking confers no insight. It culminates in tautologies. The correctness of such judgment is achieved at the cost of emptiness.

2. *Thought content and being* are uncritically *identified.* For example: "Nonbeing is not"; therefore it is in a certain sense, for it is thought in the "is." What must necessarily be thought has, merely by being correctly thought, demonstrated the reality of its object.

3. By thinking of true being in terms of this concept-realism, Plato *intercalates between thought and being an independent realm,* the world of Ideas. In so doing, he obscures both the empirical knowledge of things and the metaphysical insight into being. For the former is grounded in experience and the latter in immediate awareness. Concept-realism misses both, because with its free-floating concepts it volatilizes the substance of being.

The remarkable part of it is that though these objections are sound, they do not touch Plato's actual thinking. They are correct in regard to single propositions and developments, if these are considered as theorems of objective knowledge. But they do not touch Plato, because they do not enter upon his ground, and consequently do not affect the significance of dialectic for philosophizing as a whole.

On the first objection: Just as the knowledge of realities is bound to experience, so thinking in mere concepts, though subject to certain definite assumptions that can be logically defined, is also bound to the content of these assumptions, from which it extracts what is in them and thus ends in tautologies.

All logic down to modern logistics treats the question by formalizations. For example, the ambivalence of the copula "is" and the corresponding relations between subject and predicate are elucidated by means of a sign language which fixates each of the many different relations in a particular sign, so putting an end to the ambiguity of verbal language.

But all this began with Plato. He was perfectly well aware of the ambiguity of the copula "is." "The become is become and the becoming is becoming and the future is future and the nonbeing is not being—all these are inaccurate statements." Plato elaborates logical forms of cogent relations between deductions; he singles out premises, arranges a multiplicity of concepts by progressive dichotomic division from the most universal class to the indivisible individual. He raises the question of compelling correctness in general. The whole of logic down to modern logistics has drawn inspiration from him. The aim is an edifice of cogent formal relations between things.

But in Plato this logical endeavor stands in the service of something else; it is itself this something else. The question is: Has a thinking that is not a knowing any meaning? Can such thinking, as distinct from logistic formulations, disclose something else, which vanishes in logistic operations?

If we reflect on the nature of language and meaning, on the bond that attaches our fulfilled thinking to language, and on the futility or rather the limited possibility of translating word meanings into sign language, we shall be bound to conclude that the logical formulations which Plato was first to set forth in a systematic way are designed as the medium of an intention which suffuses them and which is likely to be lost when the medium is developed as such in endless logistic determinations.

Can the perennial magic of all conceptual philosophy and its futility be understood at one and the same time? Can it be that in its "void" something is awakened which falls silent if too much thought is devoted to the void itself? Can it be that something irreplaceable is actualized in tautologies through their place in the context of thought, through the moment for which they speak—but in such a way that a statement may equally well be taken as an eccentric way of saying nothing or as a deeply moving claim? Consider for example the words spoken by Max Weber shortly before his death: "The true is the truth."

Tautology is a foundering on the shoals of logical emptiness. Thinking can come to grief in contradictions and vicious circles. Plato's philosophizing awakens our ear to something which finds its expression in logical emptiness (tautology) or in logical fallacy (contradiction and vicious circle).

Dialectic is the logic of a communicable movement of thought. This movement of thought does not hold fast to its momentary content. As movement, it is itself content. It is a thinking in the realm of the incommunicable, which is manifested in philosophically communicable movement.

On the second objection: The objection is: Thinking has objective meaning only when it is related to reality through experience. Thinking is not being; it can relate to being only indirectly. Thinking that thinks it can know being as such is misleading. Thus Kant asks "whether, with the concept of something that is absolutely necessary, I am still thinking something or perhaps thinking nothing at all." To have objective meaning, thinking must be related to observation.

Plato takes up the question of the relation between thinking and being, between knowing and the known. Knowledge, he says, springs from the faculty within us that is related to true being. He touches on the question only in passing and with creative simplicity thrusts it aside by the act of thinking, by setting out to see what happens in this act and what it means in practice. But in the ensuing development, which became decisive only in the modern era, the question took on central importance. It was asked: How is knowledge possible? How is the subject related to the object? What is it that comprehends them both? How can both be the same, or if not, how can the subject know of the object? What does it mean to be an object? Can the dichotomy be overcome and how? These so-called epistemological questions as to the meaning, modes, limits of our knowledge have found many answers. There can be no question of a solution. Plato remains illuminating to all epistemologists, to those who combat him as well as those who follow him.

In opposition to this anti-Platonic objection one can ask: Even though knowledge of things in the world is dependent on experience and observation, might there not be meaning and content in a thinking that has no objective bearing on our knowledge of things in the world? Does the artless identification of thinking and being not conceal a lofty truth which recurs, if only implicitly, in every theory of knowledge?

On the third objection: The objection that Plato obscures all knowledge by intercalating a world of concepts between ourselves and being is based on the assumption that we can obtain a better insight without a medium, that we have a language that can dispense with objects. When, for example, the medium, in the form of mathematics, encounters reality through the experience of measurable quantities, the result is physics, natural science in the modern sense of the word. When the medium attempts to ascertain fundamental being through existential operations, their recollection or anticipation, the result is metaphysics.

In both cases, the outcome is not a darkening but a genuine approach to the truth, at least for beings of our kind. A direct approach is to be sought in the experience that transcends all object knowledge, but such experience becomes communicable only when it enters into the media of which we have been speaking. These media do not obscure, but in the lucidity of the thinking consciousness reveal something which without such revelation we cannot know.

It is Plato who first developed speculation on being in the grand manner, that is, with sovereign mastery of the means and possibilities. He laid the foundations of all subsequent metaphysics. Since then metaphysicians have often erred in hypostatizing the surface figures of thought. This they did because what they were looking for was a self-sufficient knowledge (known as ontology or theology) that could be taught in systematic doctrines represented as the result of philosophic inquiry. But even such doctrines not infrequently preserved some spark of Platonic transcending, that music of thought designed to confer an intimation of being.

With this in mind, we shall avoid taking any Platonic idea as an absolute. Each definite movement of his thought is part of an attempt to fashion an instrument for the communication of an independently achieved awareness of being—not of a self-sufficient body of objective knowledge. When these instruments are transformed into doctrines, the result is a dogmatic pseudo knowledge, in which the power of transcending is lost. Plato himself never denies, and often speaks of, the limits of man's knowledge and cognitive faculty; nor does he ever deny the sublime possibility of transcending. His thinking bears less analogy to scientific inquiry than to exercises in meditation. It cleanses the mind by rationality and in its operations yields a glimpse of being itself. It remains in motion. Every answer turns back to become a question. The meaning of these operations is to be sought in the discovery of something that I show my confidence in by looking for it, something wherein I already am if I am on the way to it.

Plato's philosophy never becomes a doctrine, but it is always concerned with the same thing. This same thing cannot be stated once and for all, but it discloses itself in different ways in the paths of thought that Plato inventively pursued.

The three objections we have discussed attack something of which Plato had at least a beginning of awareness, and with methods that Plato himself possessed. The sharpness of Plato's thinking bore fruit in three particular directions: logic (down to present-day mathematical, or symbolic, logic), theory of knowledge, and speculation on being (ontology).

But in Plato they form a whole, and what is Platonic is their indivisible unity. They are a whole which must indeed be broken down (into logic, theory of knowledge, and ontology), but only as a transitional stage by which to regain the old Platonic unity. For the bond between them in Plato does not signify a lack of clarity; rather, it is a reminder of what never ceases to be decisive, embracing all three fields and superordinate to them. For by itself each of the three streams runs dry because it does not comprehend its own meaning. Each of them sustains our philosophical reflection only when it begins once more to flow from the Platonic source. What has been separated belongs together in our consciousness of truth, which is at the same time a consciousness of being. Cutting apart seems to make things clearer. The particular factors stand out with greater rational clarity, but when the relation to the source, which is at the same time the goal, is lost, all that remains of logistic is the subsistence of concepts (which is nothing more than freedom from contradiction) and the reduction of everything to indifferent formal relations; nothing remains of theory of knowledge but endlessly varied pseudo insights into the relation between subject and object, both of which come to be treated as objects; and speculation on being ceases to be anything more than an ontology, dull or fascinating as the case may be, which purports to be a knowledge of being itself and tells me that I now know it. In each case, philosophy is turned into object knowledge and doctrine.

The three objections coincide with the three historic developments. In opposition to Plato, they demand the separation of the three, or they attack one of them through the others. All three succumb to the attacks to which their statements have laid them open, and only logistic remains, the triumph of a knowledge that is demonstrably correct but utterly indifferent and empty.

All the objections are based on assumptions about the meaning and pos- sibilities of cognition. They restrict it to rational thinking, but in so doing involve themselves in new confusion, because they do not carry out their own operations strictly. If Plato had started from these assumptions, he would not have made the "mistakes" that are imputed to him. But then he would have had no need to be Plato; any man's mind could have thought the same thing. And there would be no such thing as philosophy.

D. *The tension of the dialectic and of Platonic philosophizing in general:* If the good and the Ideas cannot be taught directly, they can be fostered in dialectical thinking. The illumination occurs in the thinking itself, but in a thinking that differs from the usual intellectual thinking. It occurs in a transcending of all clear determination (everything which thought ap- prehends in clear determinateness). Every transcending thought is once again transcended, until it is fulfilled in the failure of mere thinking but only through this very same thinking.

Such thinking strives toward the point where suddenly, in a single mo- ment, the good itself, true being, that which surpasses comprehension and can never be captured, is present to the insight. But is this sudden, "momen- tary" illumination really attained? Is it here, or does it remain elsewhere, entering into our existence as a mere reflection?

The fact that what is sought cannot become doctrine and that the think- ing of the philosophical existence is nevertheless expected to attain it, creates an extreme tension in the reader of the Platonic dialogues. There is an in- superable difficulty in the communication of Plato's thought: as though a promise had been made and never fulfilled. This is in keeping with Plato's statement that his actual philosophy is communicated neither in writing nor by word of mouth, but is actualized only in the moment when the spark of illumination passes between two men.

And yet this true philosophy is what we are trying to get at. The "realm beyond being," "the good," "the Idea of all ideas," "being itself"—these are words. If we wish to know what they are, we are either referred to experi- ences that are called mystical, a union with being itself; or we are told of a kind of speculation that leads through concepts, by a process of formal transcending, to the ground of all grounds; or else we are shown a wealth of images, myths, and configurations, which tell us in cipher what is. The dialectic gives all this its structure by making it flare up and vanish at one stroke.

The distance between these modes of thought and what can be apprehended by the senses or by reason and is equally valid for every mind, is obvious. In the first case (that of mystical union) Plato seems to speak of an objectless and therefore incommunicable experience; in the second, he seems to carry out empty movements of abstract logic; in the third, he seems to display images that remain images. Yet all this, which bursts into a fullness of light in moments of comprehension and through comprehension (for it cannot be held fast as a possession that is ready for use whenever one pleases)—just this is the encompassing power of being, reality itself. In Plato, it is the soul-stirring voice that overflows all speech. What seems to be nothing and vanishes on the plane of understanding becomes everything, but only in the lucidity of thinking.

The Platonic dialogues make the highest demands on us. For they deal with what sustains and illumines all things. To be sure, our enthusiasm can beguile us into supposing that we know it and can say it in so many words; or else it may seem like an emptiness, so that in the end we hold nothing in our hands. But this emptiness comes to us only because we have slipped back into merely rational and sensory life, forsaking being for the opaque reality of our existence. But if we succeed in turning from the emptiness of such realism to the fullness of light that radiates from being, it illumines everything that is present to us; it misses nothing but brings all things to themselves. And this turning around is bound up with an ascent to the place that is no place, that slips through our fingers as though it were nothing, and that acts upon everything because it is everything.

C. THE PLATONIC EROS

Plato disclosed three inseparable aspects of philosophizing: thinking as a way through the knowledge of nonknowledge to the knowledge that gives guidance; communicability as a condition of the truth that is trustworthy and binding; the dialectic of a sovereign thinking which can equally well produce all fixations and melt them down again, which is never satisfied with a provisional stopping place, but is oriented toward the One, the enduring and eternal.

In such philosophizing, our freedom and the other man's freedom are gained in an ascending movement. This is a freedom sustained and fulfilled by love. Philosophical knowledge is loving knowledge, and to love is to know. Knowledge becomes teachable in loving communication. Plato is the first philosopher of love. For him the earlier objectivizing myths of a cosmogonic Eros become mere parables, for he attains to the source in the reality of the Eros itself, that is, in the realization of the philosophical man.

Even the word "philosophy" means a movement of love, a *philein* of *sophia*. Philosophy is not wisdom but love of wisdom.

Plato's thinking has its source in his love of Socrates. No other love has ever left such a monument. Plato's Eros was real; illumined by the reality, it became a love of everything noble that crossed his path.

But as to what love is, that is unfathomable; Plato (particularly in the *Symposium* and *Phaedrus*) circles around the reality, touching on it only in myth. Love appears in many figures and fancies, but all are directed toward the One, the true, absolute love that bears men upward.

In Plato's discussions of love, sexuality is treated as origin, as symbol, and as enemy. Its enchantment is the origin, because the sight of beauty inspires recollection of the eternal and the ascent begins with sensuous beauty; but it is seduction when sexuality becomes self-sufficient, when by isolating itself it is sullied and debased. Without sensual origin there is no Eros, and thought remains empty. If the sensual Eros is self-sufficient, it paralyzes the philosophical Eros and becomes blind to it. Plato's philosophizing knows the power of sexuality and is both in league and in conflict with it. Philosophizing is in league with sexuality when, spurred by it, it attains to the source from which sexuality also arises; in conflict, when self-sufficient sexuality degrades man's nobility and so obscures his insight into the truth of being. According to the myth (in *Phaedrus*), the soul is the chariot of reason, drawn by two winged horses, the one disciplined and obedient, powerful in the ascent, the other recalcitrant, pursuing only its sensual desires, unruly, and tending downward. With its two horses, reason must reach the place where all knowledge has its goal and whence it derives its guidance, the suprasensory place.

Philosophical thinking is an upward-tending erotic enthusiasm. But in it we experience our vacillations, our ups and downs. We fall, we fail, we live anew in the movement of love. For love is like philosophy, a being-between. It is having and not having. It fulfills in nonattainment. In another myth (*Symposium*), Eros is the son of wealth and poverty, "on one and the same day he will live and flourish when he is in plenty, and also meet his death, and come to life again through the vigor he inherits from his father; but what he wins he always loses. . . ." The Eros of philosophy belongs to our temporal existence and outside it has no dwelling place. Gods do not philosophize and they do not love, for they know.

In Platonic thinking the Eros is represented now as a reality with multiple appearances, now as a symbol for the ascent to the eternal, now as the real medium of this ascending movement, now as the light that shows the way, now in the differentiation of true love from the degenerate forms of love. To speak of love reminds and awakens. Beneath the clarity of rational discussion, Plato lights up a mirror: love, in which the knower recognizes, or fails to recognize, himself. To look into this mirror can bring about the enthusiasm which first makes it meaningful to understand, to know, to live.

There are many mirrors of the modes of love along the way. A mistake is always possible. Even close to the summit everything can go awry.

4. *Special Fields of Platonic Thinking*

Platonic thinking is always full of very definite ideas and tangible observations. Plato's greatness lies no less in the wealth of his projects, the discovery of problems that have concerned men ever since, the invention of possible solutions, than in the fundamental impulses of philosophizing proper. His ideas must be set forth in relation to their specific subject matter. We shall not exaggerate the philosophic importance of these specialized problems, or say that they have an essential bearing on Plato's philosophy. But, on the other hand, we shall not, with the visionaries, deny that these same problems can be very fruitful. Plato's wealth of invention is admirable. He offers stimulus to specialized investigation and invites indispensable correction. In these fields our understanding can increase proportionately to our understanding of the subject in question. Logical problems, for example, and problems concerning the methodological foundation of mathematics are still studied in Plato today. We shall cast only a brief glance at Plato's so-called theology, psychology, political theory, and cosmology.

A. *Theology:* Plato speaks of God. The good, which in the *Republic* is compared to the sun, the life-giving Idea that transcends being, what in *Parmenides* is touched upon in the dialectic of the One, what in *Timaeus* is represented as the Demiurge, who, looking upon the Ideas, brings forth the world from the nothingness of space or matter—all these, one may say, refer to the same thing. But if we combine these statements into a Platonic theology, the thought is lost. For in each case his thinking approaches the limit in a different way, in metaphoric intuition, in a rising dialectic of concepts, in the myth of creation. In each case the thought is meaningful only in connection with the conditions of its thinking. If the thoughts are combined into an objective knowledge of God, their meaning, which lies in thinking as inner action, is engulfed in a supposed knowing of something. Plato's dynamic theology is turned into a dogmatic theology. And historically, this is what happened. The word "theology" occurs in Plato. He created the discipline and was the founder of Western theology. Aristotle made the word into a technical term. This creation of philosophy was adopted by the Christian churches and by Islam. But often the Platonic thought is scarcely recognizable in these definite, dogmatic systems.

B. *Psychology:* Before Plato, the soul was a name for a being inside the cosmos, or for a vital force. It was immortal, taking the form of a shadow, migrating into new births, or eternally tortured in hell. Thinking toward something that transcends and precedes these myths, Plato conceives the soul as what man himself is, his rational essence. He thinks of it in three-part structures (the rational, the courageous, the acquisitive soul, corresponding to the three elements in political life: the philosophers who rule, the warriors, and the working masses who nourish the community), or in the two-part division of a charioteer with two horses of different nature. He derives "proofs" of its immortality from its participation in the Idea of life, or from its self-given motion. He recounts myths about the lot of the soul in the other world. Once again, we must not combine these notions and images that run through his whole philosophizing into a theory of the soul (psychology), though they seem to offer abundant material for one. But this is just what was done by later thinkers, who in taking over Plato's philosophy reduced it to a mere collection of theorems.

c. *Political theory:* A sketch of the best possible state and another outlining the laws for the second-best state provide the content of the two longest dialogues, the first written in Plato's maturity, the second in his old age. They show how Plato's philosophical thinking moves in one with his theological and political thinking. In these dialogues the movement is between God and the specific realities of political life; they disclose a wealth of experience and an extraordinary political imagination.

In the true polis, the one supreme goal, the good of the individual man, gives rise to a perfecting of human nature. Philosophy becomes a school of rulers. As education, it becomes the foundation of a total scheme, in which each man in his place does his allotted part, while only the rulers (the philosophers) know the meaning of the whole. Knowledge of the true state and the true laws points the way to the ultimate goal, through contemplation of the prototype in the eternal world of Ideas. The sketch is a reflection of the Idea, not a program for establishing and organizing a sound practical government. This could be done only by philosophers educated in the truth. Through their ethos rooted in the eternal, they would promote the orders anticipated in the playful fantasy of the dialogues. A practical embodiment can begin only with the establishment of a government according to philosophical education of the rulers, not with the sketches misinterpreted as a program. Consequently Plato began building the government in Syracuse by educating the tyrant Dionysius, first of all in mathematics.

Laws ends with the idea of God; the founding of a religion (cult) coincides with the founding of the state. Religion is one with the aspect of philosophy that is accessible to all men, that is, the constraints to which they submit through belief, while dialectic philosophy is restricted to the rulers, who alone are capable of such knowledge.

Such thinking is not intended as a program to be carried out by a powerful despot, but as a guide to the actualization of the ethical-political-theological essence of the human community. It is followed by those who dedicate themselves to the earnestness of the task in their own actual community, who live by the norms that illumine the truth and untruth of the world around them.

D. *Cosmology:* In his old age Plato devoted a penetrating analysis (in *Timaeus*) to what seemed to interest him least of all, the universe, nature, "physiology." He gives a detailed account of the creation of the world by a Demiurge, but makes it very clear that he is merely telling a story of what might plausibly have happened, not expounding knowledge.

This cosmology is characterized by two related themes: The world is not eternal but was created by the Demiurge. It did not result from blindly operating causes, but was produced by a cause endowed with reason and knowledge. To be sure, the course of events in nature is also subject to a blind causality called necessity (*anankē*) (sprung from the nonbeing of space or of matter), but this is only a concomitant cause. Far from being the sole cause, it is subordinated to the purposive planning of a divine reason embodied in the Demiurge (in other words, causality is subordinated to teleology). An atomic theory after the manner of Democritus (but, unlike that of Democritus, conceived in mathematical figures) combines with the postulate of an all-encompassing idea to form an interpretation of natural reality. Thus a created world soul is the driving force of the cosmos, which is built from infinitesimal particles of the five elements.

We cannot but be amazed when we survey Plato's thinking in the realms of theology, psychology, government, cosmology (to which we here allude only briefly), when we consider the concreteness and subtlety, the simplicity and richness of the ideas he developed in these realms. It is assuredly unique in history that one man should have had such an abundance of creative and historically pregnant ideas, that he should have developed them with so much force and simplicity and gathered them all into a superordinate, never completed meaning which left him free, that he should never have become a captive to any of his creations or to any of his objective discoveries in special fields.

III. CHARACTERIZATION AND CRITIQUE

1. *On Plato as a Whole*

The identical background, from which all that is determinate and changing derives its light and shade, can only be adumbrated.

A. *The unchanging:* In the course of the fifty years in which Plato wrote, many discoveries were made; there was an enormous increase of factual knowledge. This was the time of the great movement of mathematical and astronomical investigation. The political upheavals brought new interests. Plato listened and took note and intervened with his ideas. In the course of his work we observe changes in the dialogue form. But contrary to the belief that great transformations occurred in the depths of Plato's thinking is the general impression he gives of something that is always identical.

Hints thrown out in earlier writings become the subjects of later ones. Exuberance and irony are still present in his latest work. A certain solemnity that we find in the dogmatic projects of the late period is anticipated in early passages.

There remains the fundamental attitude of being-on-the-way: not *sophia* but *philosophia;* not knowledge but knowledge through nonknowledge. There remain the ways of transcending which are traveled in thought: the growth toward being through participation in being. There remains the dialogue form as a means of communication, as a method of philosophizing through poetically transfigured persons. The task remains identical: to arrive at being, not through mystery or cult, but by thought, to find fulfillment and limits in thought, and at the extreme limits to find the signs pointing to that which is beyond all being; there remains the manner of coming to understanding through images and myths.

Philosophical freedom is unchanging. Thinking and speaking are the scene of growing awareness, not a communication of immutable truths. A man's thought and action are a game, particularly in communication. It is up to the other, to his partner and companion, to understand and to decide whether he is being made a fool of or whether a spark has been kindled in him.

Plato's teaching never becomes a system, and that too is unchanging. The most monumental doctrinal designs remain factors in the philosophy; they never engulf it.

What above all remains identical throughout Plato is the idea of the enduringly true, which fundamentally and essentially evades object knowledge, direct statement, or adequate formulation.

B. *In Plato themes that were later separated are held together (man and state, philosophy and science, philosophy and poetry):*

Man and state: Everything depends on man. Concern for the soul comes before all else. For every individual a turning around is necessary. It is achieved in philosophical thinking. Plato provides the groundwork for the philosophizing of the man who, thinking independently, relies on himself in the world. He can withdraw from political life, but he does so from necessity, in an attitude of expectancy and preparation.

For in Plato the idea of the true man is one with the idea of the true state. Man and state are inseparable in their striving toward the One, the *agathon,* toward a supreme guiding authority that is touched upon in philosophizing. Plato's philosophizing is political, not because he is interested in the special problem of pragmatic power, but because he considers man as a whole. But his state is not a bundle of institutions and laws and competencies; it is the reign of truth itself in the community of men, hierarchically ordered according to the measure of their philosophical knowledge. The perfect state will need no laws; actually laws, because they always say the same thing, are an obstacle to the movement toward perfection. The perfect state will be sustained by the philosophers who, in contemplation of eternal Being, know the truth for every moment of the changing world and hence have no need of laws.

This view of the indissoluble unity of man and state springs from Plato's awareness of the disastrous character of his times. He was determined to expose the prevailing confusion and falsehood and at the same time to search for a way out. His aim was to anticipate this possible way of salvation in the world of thought by grasping the eternal model, to actualize it through education and thereby, at the moment determined by divine decree (*theia moira*), to create a state through which man would be fulfilled. The state is true or false education; true education when the rulers are philosophers, so that all men gain a share in the truth appropriate to the place they occupy in the whole, though the overwhelming majority of course will never, by their own knowledge, come into direct contact with the *agathon*.

In Plato passion for the true state is one with an extrapolitical and suprapolitical philosophizing, for which polis and world sink into nothingness. Thus, in the state he outlines, the philosophers will govern only out of duty; they will take turns, so that after the practical activity that interrupts his contemplative idleness, each one will return to the most glorious thing of all, to pure knowledge. There is no more contradiction between negation of the world and the will to establish a state than between contempt of men and the desire to educate them.

Philosophy and science. Plato concerns himself with scientific inquiry, above all with mathematics and astronomy, but in such a way as to gather science into philosophizing. Plato's openness toward science is one with the supreme demand he makes on the philosophizing that transcends it. That is why association with Plato has proved an inspiration to modern scientists with their special interests as well as to philosophers themselves.

The unity of knowledge in Plato is a reminder to all who have come after him. Amid the confusion of sciences without guidance; amid the untruth of philosophy when it disregards the sciences (supposing that it can draw life from the nothingness of the mere thinking consciousness or from the nothingness of fantastic visions), his lofty thinking speaks in admonition.

Philosophy and poetry. Plato is a great poet. Literature and philosophy, today viewed as separate spheres with separate laws, are in Plato's work a unit. But it is no simple matter to grasp the essence of this unity, and it is something that cannot be repeated.

If we try to enjoy Plato's works as literature, to take a noncommittal, purely aesthetic attitude toward them, the truth of Plato is lost. What matters to him is the truth and its fulfillment. And it is in this light that we must understand what is said about poetry in the dialogues: Inspired by divine madness, poets create something they themselves cannot understand or judge. Poets communicate much that is false. They imitate not only the good and the beautiful, but the evil and ugly as well. Even Homer—though honored and crowned with laurel—is banished from the Idea of the best state. Socrates turns away with distaste from the interpretation of poetry. Different men interpret the same passages from the poets in different ways. "Reasonable men want nothing to do with such discussion. . . . Setting aside the poets, relying on ourselves, we must test the truth and ourselves."

Plato himself was a great poet, unparalleled in depicting the drama of ideas, the conflict between the powers of philosophy and antiphilosophy; a masterful inventor of situations, scenes, figures; a creator of myths. But to his mind the poet in him was purely a function of the philosopher, who must use every available means of communicating the truth. Plato's philosophy is not built on the unpredictable divine gift of madness, but on thought. Within himself he gives priority to thinking, and accordingly he claims for philosophy the supreme authority as a judge of the truth in poetry. Philosophy alone can be relied upon, and even philosophy is reliable only at the heights of its thinking.

But now it should be asked: Can philosophical truth be separated from poetry? Or is not truth itself lost in such "purification"? Plato at all events cannot be split into the poet and the philosopher. His truth would vanish. Nothing would be left but, first, a sum of propositions which taken by themselves would be incomprehensible and mutually contradictory; secondly, a charming and often moving richness of poetic perception. Plato's philosophy must be understood in the depths from which it speaks. As an inseparable whole, it towers over any attempt to reduce it to mere science or mere literature. Any separation of "philosophy in the strict sense" from "poetry" would destroy its force.

c. *Plato's greatness:* Perhaps all of us desire a vision of perfect philosophy personified by a great figure. For Plato such perfection resided in Socrates. Since Plato "the Western philosopher" stands configured in the duality and unity of Socrates and Plato. With a view to visualizing Plato's greatness, this truth that appears unique and never to be surpassed, I shall sum up what has been said:

1. Plato won independence in thinking *through thinking,* with the knowledge of nonknowledge. This power of thinking came to him through Socrates and was developed in harmony with Socrates.

In all doctrine he gains free movement. Because nothing that can be said and consequently nothing that can be thought as an object has definitive meaning in itself, Plato made himself *master of his thoughts*. He rose above dependence on any content of thought.

He attached great importance to *dialectic speculation* but recognized its failure when it strove to become conclusive and ultimate knowledge. He found its complement in the conscious language of *myth* and discovered justification of philosophy in myth; yet he overcame all mythical hypotheses in the earnestness of his play.

In the mobility of the rational, he discerned the substantial, which is not given by nature, which cannot be acquired by purposive effort but speaks in thinking itself, at the limits of thinking, from out of the thinker's freedom. It can be encouraged, obstructed, or wasted. In the groundlessness of thinking itself, we can gain an intimation of the ground.

2. This ground is manifested to Plato in the *reality* which no thinking can fathom. Crucial for all success in the world is divine decree (*theia moira*). The freedom of his autonomous thinking is grounded in a historic bond. That is why he was able to attain the autonomy of thought, which in the Sophists led directly to a rootless cosmopolitanism, and still remain an Athenian. In his indictment of his polis, he observed limits; he idealized his city's mythical past and, even while praising the qualities of Sparta or Egypt, never denied the superiority of the free intellectual life of Athens. Consequently there is in Plato an atmosphere of *veneration*, of piety, of love for his origins.

3. Plato found the fulfillment of philosophy in a philosophical life, and not, like certain later thinkers, in the self-sufficiency of an individual concerned solely with philosophy; he did not impoverish his life like the Stoic philosophers, who prided themselves in their imperviousness to joy and sorrow. Platonic philosophizing lives amid perils and setbacks in the Eros, the winged striving that rises from nonbeing to being. Plato's philosophy is the philosophy of a life of love, the love that brings forth knowledge and consumes existence, that draws men toward being. Only the shared striving of men bound by the ineffable, which alone has full certainty, is trustworthy. Ever since Plato, all Western philosophizing has been kindled by a spark of this Platonic truth of the philosophical Eros. How a man loves, what he loves and remembers, that is what he is; through his love he perceives his own true being. Dante, Bruno, Spinoza have borne witness to this fundamental truth. When a man awakens, the stirring of the source within him sets him in a motion that knows no rest, he is spurred on by dissatisfaction with everything that is not a transcending.

4. Plato's greatness is attested by the forms in which it is reflected. If he has been seen as the teacher of a system, the scientist, the poet of the myths, the autocratic founder of a state, the religious prophet of salvation, it means that there is something in him which can for a moment be interpreted in each of these ways. But none of these pictures captures him, all are exaggerations. The lifelong movement of his thinking was all-encompassing, full of tensions like life itself, ambiguous; he was an awakener, pointing only indirectly to the path and the goal, a creator of unrest.

2. *Plato's Limitations*

In his fundamental philosophical attitude and the mode of thinking arising from it Plato is unequaled. But the same cannot be said of the contents, the inventions, conceptions, projects, concrete views, and formulations of aims that he made use of along the way. To take these as absolutes is contrary to Plato's own way of thinking. In our acquisition of Plato we must not close our eyes to the limitations in his essential view of life, his political consciousness, his attitude toward science.

We find a historically objective standard in developments that came after Plato: the Biblical religion; the idea of political freedom based on it; the modern conception of universal science. Realities that he could not know, sources that were not available to him, throw light on a deficiency in Plato which gives some of his utterances an unpleasant ring in our ears. The limitation is not in his basic philosophical attitude, but partly in the materials with which he worked, partly in the frame of mind in which he approached certain realities. A fourth limitation becomes discernible by Plato's own standards when his philosophizing becomes a doctrinaire school philosophy.

A. *The standard of Biblical religion:* Biblical religion gives us the idea of a God who created the world from nothingness, and will, at the end of time, make it vanish again in the kingdom of heaven. It provides a basis for a radical knowledge of four things: the imperfectibility of beings in the world; the historicity of man; evil in human action and thought; the irreplaceable significance and value of every human soul. Let us examine Plato's thinking in these perspectives.

1. For Plato beings in the world are perfectible; thinking partakes of reality itself; *aretē* is possible. Error and wrongdoing are essentially deviations caused by the nonbeing of the matter in which becoming takes place. In principle they can be overcome. Perfection in the world, the perfect copy of the eternal Idea, is attainable. Imperfection is identified with its source, namely nonbeing. Corrosive suffering from evil, forlorn despair, the hopelessness of worldly existence as such are soul states unknown to Plato. He knew neither the abyss of nihilism nor yearning for the direct help of the Godhead. Plato accepts the problems of life and moves with equanimity along the path taking him closer to the divine. He needs no help but awaits "divine guidance." In total ruin, he sees a purely temporal, irrelevant incident in a process that has no end in time.

But another attitude is easily discernible. The scene of Plato's political thinking was an Athens which he recognized to be in a disastrous state. The suffering this disastrous state induced in Plato was one of the main motivations of his philosophy. He was not an impartial observer, but held himself in readiness. Beneath their cloak of irony, many passages in the dialogues are monuments to Athens.

2. Plato knew nothing of historicity. He knew nothing of a history in which irrevocable, eternal decisions are made, but looked calmly upon a never-ending temporal process in which what does not succeed today is someday acomplished by divine guidance. He had no awareness of the unique, concrete, historical time in which there is not a moment to be lost, in which every opportunity must be seized upon, in which men, accepting the concrete conditions, standing on the historically given ground, strive for an infinitely remote goal. Nor did Plato know the historicity of the individual man, wherein time and eternity come together in my decision and, in bond with the historically One, I take upon myself what I have become and what I have done, the lucid memory that obligates me to absolute loyalty.

This applies to the conscious development of his ideas. But Plato knows of the moment, the spark that suddenly flares up among men who have long lived together, the unanimous certainty of the truth. What Plato really was in his love of Socrates did not enter into his philosophical consciousness. He thought of this love, as of love in general, only in universal terms, and not in its historical uniqueness. In Plato's work the tension between the concreteness of dialogue and the conceptual universality of his thinking may be taken as an expression of historicity.

3. Plato has no consciousness of evil in its terrible, inevitable reality. Consequently, his psychology may strike one as superficial. To be sure, the plastic clarity of his psychological views enables him to disclose fundamental traits of psychic reality with a fine simplicity. But in so doing he recognizes only what is conscious. The unconscious is identical with ignorance. Self-examination is quickly accomplished, it never encounters the abyss of inwardness, which first opens up to the light of dialectic understanding. Plato maintains an aristocratic aloofness toward his own inner life, and passes over in severe silence anything that might be disturbing. He does not seek indefatigably to penetrate self-delusions; he does not, afflicted by the terrors within, do his utmost to dispel them; his psychology is concerned solely with the consequences of ignorance.

But here again Plato sometimes softly says something else. He knows of something more than the evil world soul that modern critics tend to interpret away. In *Gorgias,* after evil has been exorcised as ignorance, Callicles stands there in the flesh as the positive embodiment of the evil will. In *Philebus,* Plato speaks in passing of the pleasure men derive from the misfortunes of others, even of friends.

4. In his project for a state, Plato envisaged a number of startling possibilities: the abolition of marriage; the communal rearing of children; eugenics; the judgment of slaves; the banishment of the aged to the country, on the ground that they could no longer be educated; the degradation of the vast majority of the citizens to blind obedience and their exclusion from development in the striving for the *agathon*. Chronic incurable diseases should not be treated: "I think it is of no profit to a man to live if he is

physically wretched; for one who lives so must necessarily lead a wretched life." In all these notions Plato negates what even in antiquity was known as *philanthropia* and *humanitas*.

Both in its physical manifestation and in its philosophical interpretation, there is to us something dissatisfying about Plato's conception of love. The homosexual love that the Greeks took for granted is the historic setting which, though it does not impair the truth of Plato's thinking, compels us to fight off a feeling of strangeness. The philosophical interpretation concentrates so exclusively on the Idea, disregarding the historic possibility of love for a single, definite individual, that if we had only Plato to go by we should not even recognize the metaphysical love between the sexes that Biblical religion has made possible in the West. Plato's tendency to represent sexuality in general as evil bars the way to the fulfillment of carnal love as a pledge of eternity. There is no sublimation of the unique reality, and only in its eradication can the sensual promote a higher striving.

Plato's Eros knows no *agapē*, no love of man as man, no love of my fellow man. Consequently, Plato knows no human dignity as a claim of every man on every man.

B. *The standard of political freedom:* Plato's political thinking lacks the idea of political freedom that has become a historic force in the Western world since the Middle Ages. It was outside Plato's horizon. The seeds disclosed in Solon's legislation were wasted in the ensuing period and, even by the advocates of the mixed form of government, the idea of political freedom was never again clearly expressed.

With all his magnificent powers of invention, Plato did not anticipate the free forms of government with their possibilities of development. He conceived of philosopher-kings and explained how they were to be selected and educated. He did not conceive of a government based on the communication of all men, striving in each situation to find the right solution through a legality which is itself engaged in a continuous lawful transformation. He gave no thought to the means (e.g., representation) of creating a bond between the will of all men and the will of the rulers and their elites. He did not find a way to overcome the rigidity of the laws. It did not occur to him that this might better be accomplished, not by a superhuman philosopher-king standing above the law, but through laws susceptible of correction by legal methods which could themselves be corrected. Plato played no part in the venture of the peoples who have attempted to guide political reality through free communication and the education of all men, in such a way that no individual, however great, can enduringly take all the decisions on himself, since even the greatest of men remains a man, needful of checks and balances.

Plato did not enter into practical politics in response to actual situations, but waited for the emergence of a political reality that might serve as material for his philosophical construction of the true state. Instead of letting the laws develop from concrete tasks through the participation of the community, in a state perpetually changing in accordance with justice and legality, Plato drafted laws for an immutable state. The leap from the eternity he discerned in his philosophizing to the existential reality of a unique, irrevocable history did not take place. Plato elucidated profound impulses, perceived lofty norms, but he failed to see the necessity of a bond with the reality given here and now, in space and time. This limitation, as Plato himself understood, made his ideas inapplicable. Yet these same ideas made possible the growth of an area where political impulses could spring from the political ethos grounded in God.

It has to do with this limitation of his political thinking that Plato, thinking unhistorically, could so easily neglect the present tasks of concrete political reality, preferring a philosophical retirement from the evil world. Since historical continuity did not enter his field of vision, he felt that the ideal could at some moment or other in the infinite course of time be realized by "divine decree" (*theia moira*). There was always plenty of time, and someday perfection would set in. This was all that mattered. He gave no thought to political action within the realm of the possible, to the education of men in the art of living together through the ethos of a democracy. To be sure, he saw the problems which for every democracy remain problems. But in conceiving the ideal prototype, he saw only the authoritarian and totalitarian solution, which in his hands developed grotesquely inhuman features. Though the speakers in the dialogues represent it as a state to be founded intentionally, he did not actually see it in this light, knowing that for lack of philosopher-kings any such project was doomed to failure. But Plato devised norms which were a great inspiration to political thinking and even took on a partial reality in certain aspects of the medieval Catholic Church.

Plato can be credited only with the idea of personal freedom based on philosophical reason, and not with the idea of political freedom.

c. *The standard of modern science:* The term "science" (*epistēmē*) means something very different in Plato from what it does in the modern sciences. For Plato science is the true thinking in which man himself becomes different, in which he comes to resemble the divine—for us it is a compelling insight which involves only the understanding and leaves the man himself outside (the "private" and "personal" has nothing to do with it); in Plato it is a profound satisfaction, while in modern science, in the endless progress which merely creates steps for successors to stand on, which leaves men dissatisfied unless they can content themselves with the work itself, with the business of advancing into uncertainty, there remains the unanswered question: To what end?

In the Academy, Plato not only took an interest in the contemporary scientific movements of mathematics, astronomy, medicine (in which beginnings were made toward modern science), but took part in them with his questioning. He used them as the material of his philosophizing. He employed their findings in the scientific myth of the building of the world in *Timaeus;* their methods were for him guides for the practice of purely conceptual thought as a preparation for the transcending movement of the dialectic. He despised mere empirical knowledge.

What he regarded as essential in astronomy was not the knowledge itself but that it disclosed a reflection of the Ideas. He dismissed as useless play such experiments as those designed to clarify the relations between musical tones and strings of different lengths. He was not interested in exact empirical observation.

Plato took no pleasure in the infinite diversity of phenomena, the study of which had been the constant preoccupation of the Ionian scientists whose endeavors culminated in Democritus and Aristotle. The scientific spirit of endless progress spurred by the fascination of actual facts was alien to him.

Consequently, the Platonic Academy was not a place of scientific investigation. The notion of a compendious science, uniting all the sciences, regardless of where they had sprung up, and striving, independently of philosophy, to assemble and to foster compelling insights, was far removed from Plato. He would have had no interest in the immense work of collecting, the morphological classification of ideas and natural phenomena carried on in Aristotle's school. For the Platonic Academy was a school of philosophizing. Its central concern was to educate and form future statesmen. The men of the Academy were prepared, if the occasion offered, to seize the opportunity to found a philosophical state. They had no taste for mere learning of the kind that flowered so magnificently in the Alexandrian period.

Science and philosophy are not separate. A science that is not drawn into philosophizing has no value. This is the basis of the enduring truth that an interest in science is fundamentally philosophical and cannot be grounded in science itself, that accordingly a philosophical attitude underlies all true science. However, it never became clear to Plato or, with few exceptions, to other thinkers of his time that scientific knowledge has its own character of truth.

D. *The Platonic standard, the dogmatic tendency:* Lack of clarity concerning the relation between science and philosophy, and concerning scientific possibilities in general, is related perhaps to another tendency in Plato, though this was a tendency that never became dominant because it was fundamentally transcended in his philosophizing. I am speaking of the tendency toward conclusive dogma, the shift from fluid ideas to a congealed Idea of being, from a playful reading of signs to an externalized objective knowledge, from experimental thinking to the finished product of thought.

In Plato's clear statements on literature, lecturing, teachability, communicability, the tendency is only indicated. But as his ideas were worked out in the course of his writing, indication inevitably gave way to definite assertion, demonstration, postulation. The ideas themselves pressed him to exchange dialogue for dissertation (as in the late works), though there always remained an element of suspensive dialogue that distinguishes everything we know to have been written by Plato from what he is thought to have said in his late lecture "On the Good" (Wilpert). Here the striving for unity, actualized in present existences by the freedom of endless thinking oriented by the one guiding principle, the "good," froze into an ontological construction of being. The philosophizing with which Plato had broken through dogmatism was to end in a new and different dogmatism.

But though in his lectures Plato, the liberating philosopher who had broken through dogma, was carried back to dogma by thinking itself, it was only in the measure necessitated by the situation of his school. He founded a school of philosophizing, and in it, inevitably, there developed a school where the master taught and the student learned. It could only have been otherwise if every student had been a Plato. But now Plato was overwhelmed by the demands of his students and also by the teachable results of his own thinking. Hence the change from the early Socratic dialogues and the classical main works with their magnificent freedom to the later works which are still wholly Platonic in their sovereign mastery of thought and their dialectic invention, but which give greater scope to the didactic. It is a historical phenomenon of the first order that the most unschoolmasterlike, most indirect of philosophers, a philosopher rooted in personal uniqueness, should at the same time have been the first effective founder of a school.

Perhaps a comparison with Socrates will show that the limitation imposed on Plato by his school was inevitable. Socrates did not write or teach. Without Plato we should have known nothing about him. Plato wrote and taught and thus encountered the contradiction between the content of communication and the fact of communicating. Is there something inherently impossible in the very nature of philosophizing?

3. Plato's Significance for Us

Plato for the first time saw man in the situation of total disaster that arises through his thinking if it is false and fails to understand itself. Accordingly Plato sets the task of a radical turning of the mind. Since, with the great Sophist movement, thinking had started on the way of enlightenment, since all traditional beliefs had been shattered by Sophist criticism, since thought by its very nature and the conditions of men's life together seemed to lead to chaos—in view of all this it was necessary to seek the right way through thinking itself, with the instruments of the very same thought that was leading to such disaster. In Plato we see the first great movement of thought against the dangers and falsifications of enlightenment, but by way of increased enlightenment, by way of the reason that transcends the perversions of the understanding.

This recurrent conflict takes its first historic form in the Platonic antithesis between Socrates and the Sophists. It is the conflict between philosophy and unphilosophy, between earnestness in bond with the source and the arbitrary thinking that knows no bond. The antiphilosopher who comes into being along with philosophical thinking, and like a Proteus in a thousand disguises has accompanied it throughout history down to our own day, is for the first time consciously challenged by Plato. In this struggle with its adversary philosophy comes for the first time to itself. Plato became the source of philosophy in the crisis that never ceases even though it may be denied or talked away.

It is a fearful irony that Socrates should have been convicted as a Sophist by an Athenian court, a distortion that characterizes the situation of philosophy in the world. For the undiscerning, Socrates and Sophism were the same. Invisible to the general public, the new, the great countermovement and rebirth, was embodied in this one man. To the public he was the very essence of the Sophism they hated. The public mind, defending itself against enlightenment and the demands of philosophy, condemned him as evil incarnate. In their frivolity, the Sophists are at once irritating and acceptable to the crowd. For the Sophists are pliable, affable, serviceable, and sometimes pleasingly seductive. But when it is a question of thinking in earnest, when an absolute is manifested, an eternal truth that makes a claim on independent thinking, then there is something in man that rebels against the rigors of responsible self-clarification. He does not want to wake up but to go on sleeping.

But did Plato show the way? Does he still show us the way? The essence of his communication is to make men aware of the necessity of finding the way, and to give them the strength to search for it. The way itself is not manifested in definite instructions. For it cannot be indicated by pointing to a finite goal in the world. That is Plato's indispensable contribution to the self-responsibility of human thinking (though Plato restricts responsible thinking to philosopher-kings).

The philosophizing reader of Plato is spurred to transcend anything that may look like a doctrine. And in this transcending there is a peculiar philosophical satisfaction. The essential always seems near at hand, hence Plato's great force of attraction. It is never definitively present, hence the great demand to devote new powers to it. Plato seems to promise the extraordinary. But to attain it the Platonist must draw it from himself. Plato brings us philosophizing, which by its very nature is never completed or concluded.

In Plato we seem to see the incarnation of philosophizing as such. By his reality, we ascertain what philosophy is. Through him we test the value of our own thinking.

IV. INFLUENCE

Plato's place in the history of philosophy is unique: he stands between the Pre-Socratics with their profound intuitions of being, their naïve boldness, their monumental visions, and the Hellenists with their didactic, interpretive, dogmatic systems, which became the philosophies of individuals reduced to impotence in the new bureaucratic empires. Plato is the unique summit of farsightedness and clarity. With him, for one brief moment, the world seems to open.

Since Plato there have been Western philosophers. The Pre-Platonics, like the philosophers of China and India, lived in the axial age.* Plato took a step beyond it. What is the new factor? It is the opening up of nonknowledge by way of knowledge, but not in the mere rudiments of a briefly spoken maxim which, though implying everything, develops nothing. For Plato follows the paths of definite knowledge and, through the process and content and limits of such knowledge, attains for the first time a fulfilled nonknowledge. It is through the inexhaustible richness of the world that this philosophizing leads to being.

Plato gave to philosophy its widest scope. He opened up new possibilities and stamped it with the idea of unity. This unity is not the synthesis of all knowledge in a whole, but the essence of Plato's thinking, oriented toward the transcendent One. He assimilated the whole past, and knew himself to be a link in the chain of philosophers, but at the same time the founder of what first gave the chain its binding character and made it, properly speaking, a chain. Through him who looked back at his predecessors in the light of the spiritual present, philosophy became a lasting process. Since Plato all philosophers have been born into what he initiated.

Nearly all the themes of philosophizing converge in Plato and spring from Plato, as though philosophy began and ended with him. Everything that preceded Platonic thinking seems to serve it, and everything that came after seems to interpret it. Nevertheless, earlier philosophy is not a preparatory stage but an independent force. And subsequent philosophy is not an unfolding of Plato but independent experience of world, man, and God. But for all philosophy a moment comes when it is mirrored in Plato and tested by Plato. Yet there are two currents of Platonism: the one is characterized by submission to definite doctrines and views; in the other, philosophical freedom grounded in earnestness is gained by association with Plato. Perhaps the first, which is historically visible, preserves a vestige of the hidden life which truly thrives in the second, scarcely discernible current.

---

* In *The Origin and Goal of History* (Yale, 1953), Jaspers speaks of an "axis of world history" that passes through the fifth century B.C. in the midst of the great spiritual creativity between 800 and 200 B.C.—with Confucius and Lao-tzu in China, the Upanishads and Buddha in India, Zarathustra in Persia, the Prophets in Palestine, Homer, the philosophers, the tragedians in Greece. (Ed.)

In Platonism, Plato often acquires the authority of a master; he becomes a figure more compatible with Pythagoras than with the true Plato. The school turned its founder into the divine Plato, and the seal was set on this development by the sacrifice of the Platonic *eleutheriotēs,* freedom in dealing with ideas and projects, an inner unconstraint, liberality.

Such is the richness of thematic contents that there are few later philosophies in which Plato is not somewhere present. Thematic narrowing has turned the myths of immortality and punishment in hell into a literal doctrine of the other world; the sketch of the cosmos and creation into a natural philosophy; the theory of Ideas into an ontology and epistemology in the doctrine of two worlds; the doctrine of the Eros into a foundation for mystical enthusiasm; the projects for a state into a political program. Partial positions were turned into dogmas. Experimental probings, valid while they remained voices speaking playfully and indirectly, were transformed into a geography of supposedly known worlds. Possibilities became realities. The lucid philosophical Eros gave way to an illusory edification.

But Platonism also included a scientific impulse that pressed in the opposite direction. What Plato attempted dialectically in deductive constructions, his challenge which led the mathematicians to the path that found its didactic culmination in Euclid, was taken by thinkers from Proclus to Spinoza as a form for metaphysical speculation, and was worked out as pure form by modern logicians. Metaphysics and logical-scientific knowledge could equally invoke Plato as their source.

A Platonist can no more be defined than a Christian. The history of Platonic thinking encompasses such heterogeneous themes as Neoplatonic mysticism and Kantian purity in the self-understanding of reason, Gnostic enthusiasm and scientific clarity. But all seem to have something in common that sets them off from those who are opposed to or untouched by Plato, who reject or praise him as a poet, utopian, political reactionary, or who embody the arbitrary unseriousness, the faith in hard material facts, the nihilistic unbelief that he himself portrayed.

Let us briefly outline the history of Plato's influence:

A. *Academy:* Plato made his influence felt through his school, the Academy. In his lifetime this was a meeting place of independent personalities from all over the Greek world, particularly mathematicians. For twenty years Aristotle belonged to the Academy. It has been regarded as a school of doctrine and systematic investigation which provided the background of the dialogues. According to this theory, the dialogues are exoteric writings based on the esoteric doctrines of the school. It seems more likely that the dialogues are idealized versions of the finest conversations that took place at the Academy. The Academy was the scene of the real conversations from which Plato derived his extraordinary experience of scrupulous dialogue, of the possible perversions of discussion, of personal friendship based on common intellectual interest, of the different kinds of opposition and estrangement, and above all, of the success or failure of philosophical striving.

The Academy was to develop many forms inappropriate to the Platonic spirit. It lies in the very nature of a school that an utterly un-Platonic spirit triumphed immediately after Plato's death. Speusippus and Xenocrates introduced a dogmatization in which all independent philosophizing was lost. Aristotle left and founded his own school based on free research, but abandoning the Platonic spirit. In later generations, the so-called Academic Skeptics even transformed the freedom of Platonic thinking into a lifeless dogma. Yet the school preserved an extraordinary mobility and the power to produce outstanding philosophers of many different kinds. It flourished for almost a thousand years, until A.D. 529, when it was forcibly closed.

B. *Aristotle:* The question of the relation between Plato and Aristotle has been alive for more than two thousand years. The answer has determined the nature of each epoch's philosophizing. The conflict between Platonism and Aristotelianism has been real and radical. But there has also been, as the third possibility, the belief, and an attempt to prove, that the two were fundamentally one.

This unifying attitude turns in favor of Plato when Aristotle is invoked only in support of logical forms and specialized sciences. It turns in favor of Aristotle when Plato is regarded as a mere precursor, while Aristotle is held to offer, in purer and clearer form, what Plato, the poet and thinker in one, professed in an eloquent but rudimentary way, making mistakes that Aristotle set straight—all this in line with the opinion of Aristotle himself, who had called Plato's style a mixture of prose and poetry.

The divergence between Plato and Aristotle is clear, and every philosopher since their time has had to decide for one of the three ways. From the Platonic standpoint we may say this:

As to Aristotle, Socratic-Platonic thinking lay outside his field of vision. With all his breadth of understanding this was one thing he did not understand though, having been moved by it in his youth, he felt himself to be a part of it, but this was a matter of mood far more than of thinking. His critique, for example, of the proposition that virtue is knowledge and that no one can knowingly commit injustice, or of the Ideas that exist independently, outside of things, is always plausible and even conclusive. But it utterly misses the essence of Plato.

Aristotle was the first to classify Plato's thinking according to its place in the history of philosophy: "Next came the doctrine of Plato, which derived in the main from the doctrine of the Italic school [Pythagoreans], but also had something of its own," namely what came from Cratylus and Socrates. In answer to this classification, we may ask whether it is possible to understand Platonic thinking by subordinating it to any objective norm. "Theorems" from Plato's work can be treated in this way, but not the philosophy itself. The higher vantage point from which Aristotle classifies it is his own philosophy, a mere philosophy of the rational that sets itself up as an absolute. What it does not see it treats as nonexistent. In judging Platonic thinking, Aristotle must first reduce it to a rational statement within the grasp of his philosophy.

c. *Neoplatonism:* Neoplatonism, founded by Plotinus (c. A.D. 203–270), is the form which Plato's thinking, losing its original character, assumed for late antiquity and the Middle Ages. For more than a thousand years Platonism was Neoplatonism rather than Plato. The active aspect of Plato was submerged in contemplation. Plato's sober hardness, his either-or was blunted; the cleavage (*tmēma*) was bridged over in the doctrine of degrees; the cool Eros was lost in mysticism and finally in magic. Now philosophy claimed to be a religion. It preserved its independent existence, but the philosopher became the "hierophant of the whole world" (Proclus, 410–485).

It never occurred to Plato that he had founded a religion. But he had. Proclus filled in the frame of Neoplatonism with all the gods of late antiquity and created a Greek theology; Origen peopled the Platonic area with Biblical and Christian figures and, aided by Plato, founded Christian theology. In this, Proclus and Origen are akin, and it was from the Greek theology of Proclus that the Christian Pseudo-Dionysius the Areopagite (c. 500) largely derived his ideas.

Augustine was a Neoplatonist. He transformed Plato's Demiurge, who made the world from the matter of space, into a Biblical Creator who called it forth from the void, transformed the Ideas into the thoughts of God from whom the Logos emanates, replaced self-liberation through thinking by redemption from original sin through grace.

D. *Platonism in the Middle Ages, the Renaissance, and the Enlightenment:* The Platonism of the Middle Ages, from Scotus Erigena and the Chartres school to Meister Eckhart and Nicholas of Cusa, is in large part Neoplatonism, derived from the pagan Proclus by way of the Christian Dionysius and translated into Latin by Erigena. Beginning with the twelfth century, the *Timaeus,* a part of the *Parmenides,* and later the *Phaedo* and the *Meno* became known. It was only in the fifteenth century that the *Republic* and the other dialogues came to light.

In the Renaissance, the Florentine Academy centered around Marsilio Ficino honored Plato as the man' who had combined the two ways of beatitude (Iamblichus), that of the philosopher and that of the priest. For Ficino he was the acute dialectician, the pious priest, and the great orator. The medieval tradition was enriched by the new knowledge of all the dialogues, but no radical break occurred and a knowledge of the true Plato was not achieved. Later, in the seventeenth century, the English Platonists, Cudworth and More, took part in this movement. Love and the Beautiful took their place among the old religious contents.

On Kepler and Galileo, Plato exerted an entirely different influence— based on *Meno, Theaetetus,* and *Sophist.* It was from him that they drew their impulsion toward a new, modern, mathematical science of nature, contrary to the prevailing Aristotelianism. Leibniz first gave conscious attention to the true Plato, distinguishing him from the Neoplatonism that had overlaid Platonism for fifteen hundred years. The Enlightenment created a new Platonism concerned with educational theory and practical life: the aesthetic Platonism of Shaftesbury (1671–1713) and Hemsterhuis (1721–1790) was an important influence on German classicism. Franklin (1706–1790) found in Plato's dialogues a model of how men should talk together; he followed it in helping to lay the foundations of American public life.

E. *Nineteenth century and present:* The nineteenth and twentieth centuries (from Schleiermacher to Jaeger) achieved an unprecedented critical and systematic knowledge of the historical Plato. Now perhaps his unveiled reality will gain acceptance. Or will this historical knowledge also seep away, swallowed up by endless trifling, so that Plato's influence will temporarily come to an end? Have we still any knowledge of Plato's freedom and breadth and richness, of his impartiality and clarity, of Plato as a momentary height rapidly abandoned even in his own time? And can this knowledge remain mere information that plays no part in our own reality?

AUGUSTINE

I. LIFE AND WORKS

1. *Biography*

Augustine was born in 354 in Tagaste, a small Numidian town in North Africa. His father, Patricius, was a pagan and a lesser official; Monica, his mother, was a Christian. He acquired a classical education in his native city and later in Madaura and Carthage. As a young man he led the licentious life of a pagan. In 372 an illegitimate son, Adeodatus, was born to him. In 373, when he was nineteen, Cicero's *Hortensius* inspired him with a passion for philosophy. He became a Manichaean but in 382 perceived the untruth of Manichaean thinking. He taught rhetoric with considerable success in Carthage, Rome (382), Milan (385). Under the influence of the great Roman Christian Ambrose, Bishop of Milan, he became a catechumen in 385. In 386 he gave up his post as a teacher of rhetoric, and went with his mother and son to live in the country home of a friend at Cassiciacum, near Milan, where he devoted himself to philosophy. In 387 he was baptized by Ambrose. Shortly before his return to Africa, his mother died at Ostia. In 388 he went to Africa, where he spent the rest of his life. In 391, at Hippo, he was consecrated priest "against his will" by Bishop Valerius, and in 395 he became Bishop of Hippo. From this insignificant diocese he exerted a world-wide influence.

As a boy, Augustine had experienced the anti-Christian reaction under Emperor Julian the Apostate and the restoration of Christianity by Theodosius, who had abolished the pagan cults. He was in his prime when Alaric sacked Rome. Augustine died during the siege of Hippo by Genseric's Vandals in the year 430.

2. *The Writings*

The eleven folios of Augustine's works are like a mine. The jewels and veins of gold are embedded in great masses of barren rock. It is in the midst of endless repetitions, interminable streams of rhetoric, that we find the succinct, self-contained, classical pieces. To study the work as a whole is a life task for specialists or monks. It is as though Augustine had written every day and the reader required as long a life to read his work as he took to write it.

All the writings we possess postdate the great personal impression of Augustine's meeting with Ambrose, his conversion and abandonment of the teaching of rhetoric. The earliest of them grew out of his philosophizing with his friends in Cassiciacum. The first group consists of philosophical writings, all dialogues; Christ is rarely mentioned and there are few Biblical quotations. But his Christian conviction was real and final. Even after his baptism he wrote largely in the philosophical style until his ordination (387–391). Then began the great body of work that was to continue for the rest of his life: the sermons and letters, the exegetic works (particularly on the Psalms and St. John), the didactic writings (*On the Instruction of Novices, On Christian Doctrine,* the *Enchiridion*) and side by side with these, the great works, three of which are of particular importance: 1) *The Confessions,* c. 400; here Augustine gives praise and thanks to God by way of an autobiography in which philosophical and theological thoughts appear as the substance of a life that knows itself to be under God's guidance. 2) *On the Trinity (De Trinitate),* a profound, purely speculative work (c. 398–416). 3) *The City of God (De civitate Dei,* 413–426), the great justification of Christianity after the sack of Rome by Alaric, and at the same time a general exposition of Christian faith and historical consciousness. The polemics, first against the Manichaeans, and later against the Pelagians and Donatists, may be regarded as a group by themselves.

II. FROM PHILOSOPHY TO KNOWLEDGE

BASED ON FAITH

1. *The Conversion*

Augustine's thinking is grounded in his conversion. His mind had been impressed in childhood with the Christian conceptions of his mother, Monica, but his father had directed his education and choice of career according to the pagan tradition. His life as a pagan brought him the love of earthly existence, sensuous exuberance—and shallowness. At nineteen he was drawn to philosophy; he strove for a knowledge that would lead him from the surface of things to the essence. The path of Manichaean-Gnostic pseudo knowledge brought him to skepticism. Plotinus helped him to take the great step: to discern a purely spiritual reality and cast off the fetters of mere corporeal existence. The new insight cheered him, but he was still dissatisfied. Life did not change. His conversion was the turning point. He was thirty-three years of age. It came suddenly, after inward pressure and long hesitation. The Christian seeds of his childhood had opened, but it took them a long while to burst through.

Immediately after his conversion Augustine went to live with friends on a country estate at Cassiciacum near Milan. Here, in secluded peace, the friends met each day in earnest discussion of the question of truth. Their medium was the world of classical culture (they read and interpreted Virgil among other authors). In the early writings something of the force of ancient philosophizing seems to be reborn: we perceive the ancient passion for clear thinking. But there has been a change. These early works disclose an ancient philosophy that seems to have lost its original vitality and become an empty idiom in which the young Augustine could no longer think any fundamental or satisfying idea. A great new spiritual reality had dawned, bringing to philosophy new blood without which it would have died. What was new, characteristically his own, and objectively original came to Augustine only with Christianity; it came to him as a Christian but remained in the area of rational thinking, which he strove to deepen. Even in the writings both elements are clearly present. But the great recasting of philosophical thought was still to come.

Conversion was the foundation of Augustinian thinking. In conversion is born the sure faith, which no intention or constraint can induce, which no teaching can communicate, but which is given by God. There is some part of all thinking grounded in conversion that must remain forever strange to those who have not themselves experienced conversion.

What did the conversion mean? It resembles neither Augustine's earlier awakening through Cicero nor the joyous spiritualizing of his thinking through Plotinus, but something essentially different both in nature and in consequences. The consciousness of a direct encounter with God transformed the very heart of his existence, all his impulses and aims. After vain attempts at asceticism, it was only now that Augustine's carnal lusts were extinguished. And conversion brought him the certainty of standing on solid ground—the Church and the Bible. Now all that mattered was obedience to God, interpreted as obedience to the authority of the Church. The consequence of the conversion was baptism. But with baptism the authority became unshakable for Augustine and his celibacy final.

Such conversion is not the philosophical turnabout that must daily be renewed, in which a man tears himself out of distortion, obscurity, forgetfulness, but a definite biographical moment, that breaks into his life and gives it a new foundation. After this moment, the philosophical transformation with its daily endeavor can continue. But it draws its force from a more radical, an absolute foundation, the transformation of his whole being in faith.

After an aimless life of vain searching, the life that Augustine calls distraction, he turned back to what in childhood, in association with his mother, he had experienced as holy, and in practical reality meant the bond of the Church. Henceforth Augustine lived in the community of the Church, which was grounded not in any universal, but in historic revelation. No longer was he a cosmopolitan individual guided by the Stoic logos, but a citizen of the City of God, guided by the logos that is Christ on the cross.

2. Transformation of Independent Philosophical Ideas into Elements of a Thinking Based on Faith in Revelation

Philosophical passion is transformed into a passion of faith. They seem identical, yet they are separated by a leap, the conversion. The essence of thinking has changed. The new faith is won by a never-ending *knowledge based on faith*.

But *knowledge based on faith* means a knowledge of the content of Christian faith. Philosophical dogma becomes Church dogma.

In this movement from independent philosophizing to a Christian, believing philosophizing, Augustine seems to be speaking of the same thing. Yet everything is suffused with a new, strange blood. A few examples:

A. From the very beginning Augustine's thinking is directed toward *God*. But the Manichaean God with His body in space, at war with the diabolical anti-God, had proved to be a fantastic myth. The Neoplatonic One fired him with its pure supraspiritual spirituality, but left his soul with a vain, consuming desire that had no counterpart in the reality of the world, that found no pledge of truth in the authority of an encompassing community. Augustine first found peace in the Biblical God who spoke to him in the Scriptures, who brought unity to a life that had hitherto been dispersed, quelled the world and its passions, and received him into a real, world-embracing community, the Church.

Now the old philosophical ideas, which in themselves were powerless, became instruments in a perpetual thinking of God, who however is brought to life in the mind by faith and not by thinking. Thinking is a way, but only one way, by which to confirm and elucidate what faith has already made a certainty. Augustine's ideas of God, detached from their ground in faith, can be worked out as independent philosophical ideas. But that is not how they are intended in Augustine, for they are guided by a faith that has become one with reason. Augustine explores all the ways of coming into contact with God through thinking. But his thoughts are held together by authority, not by a philosophical principle.

The movement of Augustine's intuition of God required that philosophy adopt the Biblical idea of God and thus become a different kind of philosophy. Nor, in this philosophical metamorphosis, did the Biblical God remain what He had been in the Scriptures. Augustine transposes the Bible to a single plane, thinking away the diversities and contradictions of Biblical texts written in the course of a thousand-year development. The Bible is his guiding thread; but it is also the anchor to which he attaches his own thoughts, confident of having found them in the Scriptures.

B. Augustine took over the *philosophy of Plotinus*. With a few changes, he thought, it would be Christian. No other philosophy had so great an influence on him. His judgments of the Stoics and Epicureans were always negative. He seldom mentions Aristotle. He had no knowledge of Plato, whom he identified with Plotinus.

He agreed with Plotinus about the fundamental structure of the idea of God: everything has its ground in God. He is *reality* and as such the source of the existence of things; as *logos,* the intellectual light, He is the source of the truth of things; as the *good per se,* He is the source of the goodness of all things. The three philosophical sciences, physics, logic, ethics, relate to Him in these three aspects. Every question, whether it concerns the world, knowledge, or freedom, brings Augustine back to God. From Plotinus he took his cosmology, the doctrine of degrees, the beauty of the world, in which evil is only a privation, a nonbeing amid the being that is always good.

But Plotinus' philosophy as assimilated by Augustine undergoes a radical transformation: Plotinus' One, beyond being, spirit, and knowledge, becomes in Augustine identical with God, who is Himself being, spirit, and knowledge. Plotinus' triad—the One that is above being, the spirit that is being, and the world-soul that is reality—becomes in Augustine the Trinity, the One God in three persons. Plotinus' One emanates spirit, world-soul, matter in an eternal cycle. In Augustine not eternal emanation, but a unique Creation is the ground of the world, which has a beginning and an end. Plotinus' One is at rest, man turns toward it. Augustine's Biblical God is an active will, which turns toward man. Plotinus did not pray. Prayer is the center of Augustine's life. Plotinus finds exaltation in speculation aimed at ecstasy, Augustine in penetrating self-examination, aimed at clarification of faith. Plotinus finds himself in a free company of individual philosophers, dispersed in the world, Augustine in the authority of the Church, in the living presence of a powerful organization.

3. The Development of Augustine's Thinking

Augustine's development has its one crisis in the conversion, but this act of conversion is repeated throughout his life and only thus completed. Consequently, Augustine's baptism is not a fulfillment but a beginning. In his writings we may follow a process by which he grew into the vast totality of Christian, Catholic, ecclesiastical existence, which he helped to make into the spiritual force of a thousand years.

The movement of Augustine's thinking springs from the tasks involved in the Church's struggle in the world. The practical and spiritual situations of ecclesiastic life supply his themes. His knowledge based on faith is clarified and defined in controversy against pagan philosophy and the heresies. Clarity brings depth. Lucid discourse leads faith to full awareness of itself. The nature of God and of evil is clarified in the polemics against the Manichaeans; freedom and grace, original sin and redemption, are clarified in the controversy against Pelagius and the Pelagians; the catholicity of the Church as the one *corpus mysticum* of Christ is elucidated in the polemics against schismatics, specifically the Donatists. And the nature of the Church is clarified in Augustine's justification of the Church against the attacks of the pagans who, after Alaric's seizure of Rome, declared that the catastrophe had been brought about by the forsaking of the old gods.

Augustine worked out his new ideas on a foundation which after his conversion remained the same. Yet we observe radical changes of position in important matters: his plea for free persuasion of the heathen later gave way to the demand for their compulsory inclusion in the Catholic Church (*coge intrare*). His doctrine of free will is almost entirely lost in his doctrine of grace. Looking back, he becomes aware of past errors. At the end of his life he wrote the *Retractationes,* in which he considers his writings in chronological order and subjects them to a detailed self-criticism from the standpoint of Church dogma. He expressly disavows his former agreement with Plotinus.

But above all, his evaluation of philosophy had changed completely. As a young man he had set rational thinking at the summit. Now he judges it disparagingly. The inner light stands higher. "Those unlearned in these sciences will give true answers, because in them the light of eternal reason is present insofar as they can apprehend it, and in it they perceive these immutable truths." Philosophy has lost its validity. Biblical-theological thinking is all-important.

III. THE MODES OF AUGUSTINE'S THINKING

1. *Elucidation of Existence and Biblical Interpretation*

A. *"Metaphysics of inner experience":* A basic trait of Augustine's thinking that proved immeasurably fertile was his perception of fundamental psychic experience. He reflected on the wonders of our actual existence.

Whatever he encounters in the world, things in themselves are without interest for him. He knows that he is in conflict with the prevailing attitude: "Here are men going afar to marvel at the heights of mountains, the mighty waves of the sea, the long courses of great rivers, the vastness of the ocean, the movements of the stars, yet leaving themselves unnoticed. . . ." His only desire, which draws everything else into it, is: "I desire to know God and the soul" (*Deum et animam scire cupio*); "Let me know myself, let me know thee" (*noverim te, noverim me*).

Augustine presses forward to every limit in order, thrown back upon himself, to hear the voice of Another within him. "Go not outward, turn inward into thyself; in the inner man dwells the truth; and if thou hast found thy nature to be changeable, transcend thyself" (*Noli foras ire, in te ipsum redi; in interiore homine habitat veritas; et si tuam naturam mutabilem inveneris, transcende et te ipsum*). Augustine's exploration of the soul is an exploration of God; his study of God is a study of the soul. He sees God in the depths of the soul, and sees the soul in relation to God.

This bond is not torn in favor of a mere psychology. Augustine has been called the first modern psychologist, but his psychology, with all its description of real phenomena, is not a science of empirical realities; it seeks, rather, to elucidate our inner action, the presence of God in our soul as the starting point of our knowledge.

The soul's bond with God is not cut for the benefit of a mere theology. Augustine's talent for speculation has been much praised, but the metaphysical, transcending movements of his thinking are not so much insights into something other as fulfillments of his own upward striving. He has been seen as a great dogmatist and accorded a leading position in the history of dogma, but his dogmas are not yet articles of faith as in later theology; they are revelations of his own emotion, expressed in rational terms. Windelband called this manner of thinking a "metaphysics of inner experience," rightly because Augustine was concerned in clarifying the suprasensory motivation in man, wrongly because the term suggests a new objective metaphysics of the soul.

Never before had a man faced his own soul in this way. Not Heraclitus ("You could not find the boundaries of the soul, so deep is its logos"), not Socrates and Plato, for whom everything depended on the good of the soul. "Man," cried Augustine, "is an immense abyss [*grande profundum est ipse homo*], whose very hairs Thou numberest, O Lord. . . . And yet are the hairs of his head more readily numbered than are his affections and the movements of his heart."

And he sums up the whole of his awe in one short sentence: "I became a question to myself" (*questio mihi factus sum*). Augustine often busies himself with everyday phenomena. He finds wonderfully simple sentences to describe in a few words things of which no one before him had been so clearly aware. He thinks in the form of progressive questioning, of questions that are not simply answered but open up a field. A few examples:

First example: memory. One of the so-called psychological phenomena described by Augustine is the way in which our own inwardness puts a world at our disposal. Endlessly we visualize things we have seen in the past, that our imagination produces. A vast inner temple stands open to me. It appertains to my nature. But such words, Augustine says, are easily spoken. They do not bring a grasp of what he is trying to communicate, which is always more than what I think of myself. And so he continues: "I say, it is a power of mine and appertains unto my nature," and yet, "I myself do not grasp all that I am. Therefore is the mind too narrow to contain itself? And where should that be which it does not contain of itself? . . . A great admiration rises upon me; astonishment seizes me." When Augustine speaks of the waves of the sea, the rivers, and the stars, he marvels "that when I spoke of all these things, I was not looking on them with my eyes, and yet I could not speak of them unless those mountains, and waves, and rivers, and stars which I saw, and that ocean which I [never saw and only] believe in, I saw inwardly in my memory in the same vast dimensions as I saw them outside myself."

Second example: self-certainty. Augustine was first to express the thought, which he couches in a number of forms, that all doubt in the truth is dispelled by the certainty of the "I am." "For even if he doubts . . . he understands that he is doubting. . . . A man may doubt everything else, but he should not doubt any of these facts; for if they were not so, he could doubt of nothing" (*De Trinitate*). Thus doubt in itself demonstrates the truth: I am if I doubt. For doubt itself is possible only if I am.

Now the question arises: What is the content of this certainty? In Augustine it is not an empty observation made once and for all, but the outcome of a reflection that is never concluded. The certainty that arises in extreme doubt has more to offer than a feeling of existence. Self-certainty shows me not only that I am, but *what* I am. The following dialogue is a beginning of progressive questioning:

Thou who wilt know thyself, knowest thou that thou art? — I know. — Whence knowest thou? — I know not. — Feelest thou thyself to be simple, or manifold? — I know not. — Knowest thou thyself to be moved? — I know not. — Knowest thou thyself to think? — I know. — Therefore it is true that thou thinkest. — True. — Knowest thou thyself to be immortal? — I know not. — Of all these things which thou hast said that thou knowest not, which dost thou most desire to know? — Whether I am immortal. — Therefore thou lovest to live? — I confess it. — How will matters stand, when thou shalt have learned thyself to be immortal? Will it be enough? — That will indeed be a great thing, but that to me will be slight. — . . . Thou dost not then love to live for the mere sake of living, but for the sake of knowing. — I grant it. — What if this very knowledge of things should make thee wretched? — I do not believe that is in any way possible. But if it is so, no one can be blessed; for I am not now wretched from any other source than from ignorance. And therefore if the knowledge of things is wretchedness, wretchedness is everlasting. — Now I see all which thou desirest. . . . Thou wishest to be, to live and to know; but to be that thou mayest live, to live that thou mayest know.

In self-certainty, I find a perception of what is beyond all sensory perception and all knowledge of things in the world:

We possess still another sense, far above any corporeal sense, the sense of the inner man, by which we perceive right and wrong, right by its agreement with the suprasensory form, wrong by its deviation from it. This sense confirms itself and has no need of sharp eyesight.

In self-certainty I find my all-embracing, unbridled will to happiness. This will, as the above-quoted dialogue states, is love of life, which in turn is love of knowledge.

We exist, we know of our being, and we love this being and this knowledge. And in these three elements no possibility of error need trouble us. For we apprehend them, not as we apprehend the things outside us, with any bodily sense, but beyond any possibility that my fancy is deluding me, I am absolutely certain that I am, that I know it, and that I love this knowledge.

Toward what is this love, this fundamental will, directed? Augustine replies without reservation: Toward being and toward knowledge.

No more than there is anyone who does not wish to be happy is there anyone who does not wish to *be*. . . . It is only because there is something so naturally and powerfully pleasant about being that unhappy men do not want to die. . . . If they were granted an immortality in which their misery did not cease, and offered the choice of either living in such misery forever or of not existing at all, they would surely cry out for joy and prefer to live forever in this state than not to exist at all.

The fundamental thought leads from doubt in all truth to a certainty beyond all doubt. This is no empty certainty of mere being. It implies a fulfillment.

But Augustinian certainty—it seems to us—can collapse: into a mere statement of being, indubitable but meaningless; into a brutal love of any kind of life; into the emptiness of truth as mere correctness. Thus we must ask Augustine two questions: Whence comes true fulfillment? What is the meaning of these nullities?

To the question: Whence comes the true fulfillment that first lends meaning to self-certainty? or to the question: Where lies the source of concrete content as opposed to emptiness, of being-given-to-oneself as opposed to unfulfillment, of peace as opposed to the despair of groundlessness? his answer is: In God alone. Being, knowledge of being, and the love of being and of knowledge in self-certainty are grounded in God. In self-certainty as such lies certainty of God. For God made man in His image. In self-certainty Augustine discerns the image of the Trinity.

If we inquire as to the meaning of the nullities that remain when self-certainty collapses, the answer is: Since Augustine thinks everything with a view to God, so that for him what is independent of God does not exist, his thinking, because everything is created by God, can give radiance to everything, even to empty correctness as an image of eternal truth and even to lust for life as the lowest form of love of being. Untruth results only when the order of rank is reversed. What seems to be, and is, emptiness when it stands solely upon itself, becomes truth in the reflected light of these lower spheres. Augustine does not know the fundamental questions of the suicide; he does not know the despair of not wanting to live; he does not know the will to delusion, nor conscious self-deception, nor the possibility that all "truth" may be questionable.

Thus Augustinian shelteredness in God is something other than philosophical self-certainty. He lives toward the place where "our being will know no death, our knowledge no error, and our love no stumbling block." But here in time, if we are so certain of our being, our knowledge, and our love, it is not primarily "on the strength of someone else's testimony. In our very own person we feel it to be really present and perceive it with the inner eye that cannot be deceived" (philosophically, that is to say). But at the same time "we have other witnesses whose credibility cannot be doubted." Thus for Augustine self-certainty and the "other witnesses" (the authority of the Church, revelation) stand abruptly side by side. The content and fullness of the self spring from God's image in man and are confirmed by the other witnesses.

Third example: time. Augustine concerns himself with time. It is present at every moment. And the more deeply he delves into it with his questioning, the more unfathomable its mystery becomes for him.

We speak of past, present, future. "If nothing passed away, there would not be past time; and if nothing were coming, there would not be future time; and if nothing were, there would not be present time."[1] But strange: past and future are not, the past is no longer, the future is not yet, and if the present were always present, if it did not lose itself in the past, it would no longer be a time. In order to be a time, the present must exist in the fact that it passes immediately into nonbeing.

Are there three times, or only one, the present? For indeed, future and past are only in the present. When I relate things past, I regard their images in the present. When I think of the future, possible actions and images are present in my mind. There is only the present and in the present three times. The memory is present in regard to the past, intuition is present in regard to the present, and expectation is present in regard to the future.

But what is the present? What we say about long or short periods of time applies to the past and future. A hundred years, a year, a day, an hour: they cannot be present. However long they may endure, there is always something of the past, present, and future in them. If we could conceive of a time that could no longer be divided into infinitesimal particles, we should say that it alone is the present. But so quickly does this particle of time pass from the future into the past that the present has no duration. It is only a point, a boundary; in being, it is no longer.

When we measure time, we obviously do not measure the present that has no duration; we measure periods of time that become perceptible by passing. But this means that we measure what either is no longer or is not yet. With what measure do we measure the time that is not?

It has been said that the movements of the sun, the moon, the stars, are

[1] This and the following quotations are from *Confessions*, tr. J. G. Pilkington.

time. But if this movement is time, then so is all motion. If the heavenly luminaries took a holiday, it would be as though a potter's wheel had come to rest. But in any case, motion is not time; rather it is by time that motion is measured—as longer or shorter. The movements of the stars, like the turning of the potter's wheel, are signs of time; they are not themselves time. But the question under consideration is not what motion is or what the day is, but what time is. With it we also measure the circuit of the sun. And with it we measure not only motion but also the duration of non-motion.

Thus, says Augustine, I measure without knowing with what I am measuring. I measure the motion of a body with time. And yet do I not measure time? Wherewith do I measure time itself? I measure the length of poems, the feet of verses, I compare them, I perceive that one lasts twice as long as another. From this I conclude "that time is nothing else than an extension, but of what I know not."

The mind—this is Augustine's ultimate answer—is itself the extension of time. If I read a poem, I measure the syllables, but what I measure is "not themselves, which now are not, but something in my memory, which remains fixed." Thus I measure in my mind "the impression which things as they pass by make on" me and which, "when they passed by, remains. . . ." Three things are done by the mind: "it expects [*expectat*], is aware of [*attendit*], and remembers [*meminit*], so that that which it expects, through that of which it is aware, may pass into that which it remembers."

Thus the problem seems to be solved. The mind measures itself in that which is present to it. Thus it is able to measure the transient. But then it turns out that "we measure neither future times, nor past, nor present, nor those passing by, and yet we do measure times."

Augustine thinks in questions. The question: What is time? is answered by new questions. The mystery is not dispelled but brought to consciousness as such. "What then is time? If no one ask of me, I know; if I wish to explain to him who asks, I know not." "I inquire only, I make no assertions."

Augustine was driven to the question of what time is by the argument against the idea of Creation: What did God do before He created heaven and earth? If He was resting, why did He not remain in inactivity? If a new will rose up in Him, can we speak of a true eternity in which a will comes into being that was not there before? But if the will was present from all eternity, why is the Creation not eternal?

Augustine resolves this objection to the idea of Creation as follows: With the Creation, God also created time; before that, there was no time. The question is meaningless, because, for Him who created time but is not in it, there is no temporal "before." Time has a beginning, says the Bible; but there was no time before this beginning, says Augustine.

And yet Augustine himself asks: But what is the eternity that preceded all time? For a moment he attempts to compare God's eternal knowledge, which in unmoved presence is always whole, with the way in which a song we are singing is present to us, for as we sing, everything past and future in it is known to us. The centuries lie open before God as before us the song we are singing. But it is not in the same faulty way as we know the whole song, that the Creator knows the whole future and the whole past: Thou knowest "far, far more wonderfully, and far more mysteriously."

Augustine explains what eternity is by contrasting it with time. God "in the excellency of an ever-present eternity precedes all times past, and survives all future times . . . [His] years neither go nor come; but ours both go and come, that all may come. All [His] years stand at once since they do stand; . . . but [our years] will be when all will have ceased to be."

Eternity is the goal of all our striving, not something that will come only to pass away, but something immutable that lies before us. There, in eternity, is unity, permanence, beatitude, unmoving presence.

But eternity speaks even now, in the world; even here, God shines before Augustine, striking his heart, "so that I tremble and take fire—tremble in that I am unlike unto Him—take fire in that I am like unto Him."

To sum up: it is only through questioning thought that time becomes wholly perceptible as the mystery it is. But I think it in order, through this same mystery, to gain certainty of eternity, God's eternity and my own, in which time is extinguished.

B. *Interpretation of the Bible:* When Augustine moves, questioning, toward certainty in pure thought, he does not invoke revelation. His most profound speculations are a concrete clarification of existence. But his philosophizing does not understand itself as a clarification of existence or a thinking of God out of mere self-certainty; it seeks its truth in a Biblical interpretation grounded in faith. The basic thought-form of his speculation hinges on revelation. The *Confessions* are written in the form of a prayer, perpetually giving thanks and praise to God. In many texts insight is gained through Biblical exegesis or confirmed by quotations from the Bible.

The fundamental belief that the Bible is the sole source of essential truth transforms thinking. Opinion is no longer based on reason as such or on the essence of man as he is given to himself in reason, but along with reason on the Bible. Though at times Augustine gets along without the support of the Bible and arrives independently at his insights in the area of reason, he always returns to it when he is in need of answers to the abysmal, unanswerable questions that have pressed in upon him in the area of reason.

The Bible became his never-failing guide to the truth. With the help of nonhistorical methods of exegesis, this deposit of the Jewish nation's religious experience over a thousand years enabled him, through productive understanding, to uncover inexhaustible riches, to penetrate unfathomable depths.

For Augustine the Bible was the language of revelation that is the source of all truth; the philosophical idea of transcendence was fulfilled by the Biblical idea of God, which transformed speculation into living presence. The finest philosophical sentences paled before a line of the Psalms.

Reason and faith are not two separate sources that meet at some point. Reason is in faith, faith in reason. Augustine knows of no conflict that can be resolved only by the surrender of reason. A *sacrificium intellectus*, Tertullian's *credo quia absurdum* is alien to him. Hence Augustine's believing verification of the truth does not start with unequivocal Bible quotations from which dogmas are deduced. Rather, faith, as living and active presence, is in fact (though not consciously) free in its approach to the Bible as an unfathomable depth that remains to be understood. The unphilological and unhistorical methods of interpretation, developed before Augustine, made it possible to find almost any tenet of faith in the Bible. For this reason, Augustine's writings (except for the earliest) are shot through with quotations from the Bible. On the other hand, the main contents of Augustine's thinking, even if we do not share in his revealed faith, are intelligible to us because of the freedom of his operations. And then, in the area of reason, we can re-enact the secure truth of this Augustinian thought process as the elucidation of the soul's inwardness down to the limits where it transcends itself; the examination of time, memory, infinity; the disquisitions on freedom and grace, Creation and the world.

2. Reason and Believed Truth

The truth is only one. It is the "common possession of all its friends." The claim to have a truth of one's own is a "presumptuous assertion," it is "vainglory." "Because Thy truth, O Lord, does not belong to me, to this man or that man, but to us all, Thou hast called us to it with a terrible warning not to claim it exclusively for ourselves, for if we do we shall lose it. Anyone who chooses to regard it as his sole possession, will be expelled from the common possession to his own, that is, from truth to lie."

Accordingly, Augustine sets out to seek the common truth, even in the company of his adversaries. Such a quest is possible only if both parties relinquish the pretension to being already in possession of the truth. "Let none of us say he has already found the truth. Let us look for it as though we did not yet know it on either side; for we can search for it in peace and devotion only if both parties, rejecting all presumptuous prejudice, renounce the belief that it is already found and known." Here Augustine speaks wholly as a philosopher. He knows that he who desires the truth brings peace, for he goes with the other toward what is common to them, not toward conflict. Is Augustine speaking sincerely? For he *is* certain about the truth of his faith; only the particulars of its formulation can remain in doubt. Or is he speaking sincerely nevertheless? If he wishes to speak with his adversary, it is not to command, but to convince him. What arouses ideas of sincerity or insincerity in us is on the one hand an abrupt turnabout that Augustine effects over and over again: from a searching for the truth to a having-found the one truth and, on the other hand, an attitude which perpetually transforms having-found to a thinking search. This contradiction makes possible both the sternest intolerance and a readiness to meet the other halfway. The turnabout annuls communication by restricting it to limits that destroy its meaning; essentially it decides everything in advance. Let us take a closer look at it.

The question is: How shall I find, in the other and in myself, the hallmark of the particular, of that which is not common to us, hence of the lie? Though Augustine sees the truth in the common freedom of reason, in the attempt of two men to convince one another, nevertheless it is present only in revelation, Church and Bible. Hence in practice, Augustine, contrary to his earlier demands, concludes that force should be used against those of different faith. This same turnabout from open communication to the right of the sole authority to employ violence may be observed in the following: In pious thoughts, Augustine forbids setting anything else in the place of God. To see the authority of faith in the surface of things is to take too short a view. For then, "we remain standing along the way and set our hope in men and angels" (rather than in God). Not even Jesus desired to be anything else for us than a way; he demanded "that we should pass him by." Authority is only in God. Everything else is along the way and becomes idolatry if taken in God's stead. But now comes the turnabout. To the question: Where does God speak? the answer is always: In revelation. With revelation we do not remain on the way but, through the love with which God seizes hold of us, we attain to God in the faith of the Church, to which we bow in obedience.

Or the turnabout may take this form: on the way, an independent life of reason is reflected in rational endeavors. Such endeavors require justification. In De musica, Augustine declares that he would never have undertaken such a venture had the need to refute the heretics not compelled him "to sacrifice so much strength to such childish occupations as discourse and discussion." Thus thinking is an aid to those of weak faith. To do what holy men accomplished by a swift flight of the spirit required long and tedious ways on which they would not have deigned to set foot. For they worship, in faith, hope, and charity, "the consubstantial and immutable triunity of the one supreme God. They are purified not by the flickering lights of human reason but by the mighty, burning power of love." Over and over again, this deprecation of thinking and single-minded devotion to faith and love, which surpass all thought and can do without it, this sharp view of the fundamental difference between thinking and faith, results in a turnabout from thinking to faith. But though the highest, fullest truth speaks to the believer alone, though reason in its endless searching can never attain to it, still there can be no faith without reason. Therefore Augustine says: "Know in order to believe, believe in order to know" (*intellige ut credas, crede ut intelligas*). Belief, too, is thinking. To believe is nothing other than to think with assent (*cum assensione cogitare*). A being that cannot think can also not believe. Therefore: Love reason (*intellectum valde ama*). Without faith there can be no insight. Yet insight does not eliminate, but reinforces, faith.

Thus the astonishing Augustinian turnabout culminates in the coercion of those of different belief. But before that, it had led to the ideas that God Himself is heard in His revelation and that thinking and believing are one. This turnabout is a universal manifestation of the Christian world which had its greatest thinker in Augustine. Is it merely an error that we can quickly dispel with the enlightened ideas of an all-embracing reason? Were men of high stature, men able to think sharply and profoundly and to produce magnificent art and poetry, misled by a mere error? Or did philosophy itself operate under the cloak of revealed faith? Here we shall content ourselves with determining more closely what Augustine thought.

A. *Theory of knowledge:* 1) Our fundamental experience of thinking is that a light dawns on us by which we recognize the universal validity and necessity of timeless truths, such as: The sum of the angles of a triangle is equal to two right angles, or $7 + 3 = 10$. The miracle of the truth is that I know something that I do not see outside myself in space and time. How do I, a finite creature of the senses, living in space and time, come to truth of such a timeless, nonsensory, nonspatial character?

Augustine replied with Platonic metaphors and metaphors of his own: The truth *rested unknown within me;* made attentive, I draw it from my own previously hidden and still unfathomable inwardness. Or: When I discern it, I see it with a *light* that comes from God. Without this light there could be no insight. Or: There is an *inward teacher,* who is in communication with the logos, the word of God, which instructs me.

Augustine's reflection on the riddle of valid truth leads him to find God's action in valid truth. What was later unfolded in rich developments, complex distinctions and knowledge, has its historic ground in the sharp formulations which Augustine derived from various sources.

But there is one Platonic idea from which Augustine never departs: Though we see the truth in a divine light, we do not see God Himself; and: Our knowledge is no feeble reflection of divine knowledge, but different from it in essence.

2) Though the truth that we know is one, it includes several factors. *Knowledge* and *will* are both one and distinct.

Separately, knowledge is nothing; it takes on meaning only in unity with the will. The will to prove the existence of God does not arise from the mere intellect. Augustine deplores his former error of wishing to know the invisible in the same sense as he knew that seven and three make ten.

There is no knowledge of God in the soul, except through the modes by which the soul tries to know Him and knows Him not. There are riddles upon riddles: the creation of the world, the unity of soul and body. But thinking should press perpetually into them: "Know what thou dost not know, lest thou shouldst not know it at all." The summit of truth opens up only to one who enters into philosophy with his whole being (*totus*), not merely with the isolated function of his understanding. The conditions for knowledge of the truth are purity of soul, love, the worthiness that comes of a life of piety. The desire to do right comes before the desire to know the truth. He who lives well, prays well, studies well, will see God. But such insight is destroyed by intellectual pride.

B. *Revelation and Church:* The truth has reason and revelation as components. They are one and separate. God not only illumines the knowledge of the mind, but bestows the truth itself through the revelation of the present Church and the Biblical Church. Faith is ecclesiastical faith or it is no faith at all. For Augustine it is certain that God can be found only in this way. His faith is not only the fundamental experience of selfhood as being-given-to-oneself, but beyond that, an overpowering of selfhood from outside: the soul can trust in itself and in that whereby it is given to itself only if the earthly Church lends confirmation. In Augustine the fundamental and universally human experience that when I am wholly in earnest in my own action I know myself to be gripped by something that I am not, so that I and my action stand in the service of something other, takes the concrete, historical form of service in this Church.

In Augustine we can study this process at the source and on the highest level of ecclesiastical thinking. In him the possibilities sometimes seem wider, more open than at a later day, but even in Augustine they took on the very concrete forms in which the self-understanding of Church power was to develop.

c. *Superstition:* Augustine despised the sciences. He held that concern with them is rewarding only insofar as it promotes understanding of the Bible. For him the world was without interest, except insofar as the creation points to the Creator. It is a place of parables, images, traces.

Although the ancient books were still available, Augustine's age had almost forgotten the sciences, which had ceased to develop in the last century before Christ. We see Augustine in conflict with superstition and himself caught up in superstition. For to his mind superstition supported by the Bible was no superstition. And the crucial argument against superstition was not better, methodic insight into the realities of the world, but belief in God and the striving to save one's soul. Accordingly, we find nearly all the superstitions of his time strangely intermingled in his work.

In his polemics against the Manichaeans he used reasoned arguments. He strove to confute their alleged knowledge of the cosmos, the stars, cosmic processes, the struggle between two cosmic powers, by considerations accessible to the understanding. His indictment was: "They made me believe blindly." He saw through the unreason of their pseudo knowledge.

In this rejection of pseudo knowledge as superstition lies the power of his belief in God, his hostility to occult knowledge, magic, and charlatanism. This belief in God made for honesty and openness. But then Augustine came to feel that none of this worldly knowledge, whether true or false, is the saving knowledge that helps the soul. His use of reasoned arguments against it, however, bears witness for a moment to his inclination for scientific, that is to say, logical, methodic, empirical investigation, and for the distinction between the knowable and the unknowable. But this feeling is present only in fleeting ideas that are not held fast by method. It is quite unreliable. For in many questions concerning realities in the world, to which a science can provide universally valid answers, Augustine on the basis of Christian faith makes assertions which, on scientific grounds, draw from us the same verdict as he delivered against the pseudo knowledge of the Manichaeans. His belief in God did not prevent him from putting forward a pseudo knowledge similar to theirs, though in different contexts.

I shall cite an example which at the same time shows the profundity of Augustine's thinking. He combated astrology as a superstition dangerous to the salvation of the soul. Some of his arguments are perfectly sound and still valid today. But then he goes on to observe that since many men have succumbed to this superstition, it must be considered as a reality, and, moreover, that astrological predictions are sometimes accurate. How is this to be accounted for? Augustine's answer: By the existence of demons. In the lower regions of the air there live evil angels, servants of the devil. They gain power over those men who lust for evil things and deliver them over to mockery and deception. In themselves, these delusions have no force or reality, but "because men concerned themselves with these things and gave them names, they first acquired power. Hence, for each man something different comes from one and the same thing, according to his ideas and assumptions. For the spirits, scheming deception, provide each man with the very thing in which they already see him entangled by his personal assumptions."

Augustine takes the existence of the demons for granted. They are not superstition, because the Bible speaks of them. In the statements of the superstitious the demons may prevail. But the deception is dispelled when truth triumphs in the life of one who believes in the one God. Thus the demonic reality is combated, not by reasoning, but by the reality of the ethos. Superstition, the reality of the demons, and a life of darkness are linked, just as faith is linked with the reality of God and the ethical life. It is not reasoned insight, but faith that decides. Superstition is the act by which I enter into a pact with the demons.

Augustine's entire work is shot through with the superstition known as "popular piety." As an active priest, he accepted every existing popular belief: hell, purgatory, the cult of the martyrs, relics, the intercession of the saints. He writes with evident delight that "all Africa is full of the corpses of saints." He believed uncritically in all sorts of miracles. But to all this we can oppose his magnificent and often repeated definition: superstition is the worship of a creature as God. His failure to uphold this true and lofty standard is the source of the many contradictions in his work, which indicate that in practice neither Augustine nor the believers of his time observed the distinction between God and creature. (And indeed this has been true throughout the greater part of Christian history, applying also to Luther and many other Protestants, who combated the superstition, the belief in devils, witches, miracles, that they themselves carried on.)

In dealing with concrete problems, subject to scientific investigation, Augustine loses himself in farfetched, unmethodical, frivolous disquisitions. Smatterings of scientific knowledge, rationalistic argumentations, phantasmagorias are the dark fog that permeates his work. But the mists are dispelled where the true Augustinian ideas rise in grandiose clarity, as though to a higher realm.

3. *God and Christ*

Augustine's Christian intuition of God moves in two directions. It reaches out beyond any provisional existence, so that God becomes increasingly unfathomable, remote, and distant. But at the same time, He becomes wholly actual, corporeally present in Christ: God became man and is infinitely close to us in the Church, which is the mystical body of Christ. In the first movement, God seems to move out into the boundless; in the second, He comes home to us.

Augustine's God is inseparable from Christ, the unique revelation of God, to which the Church bears witness. That is the meaning of conversion: to find God by way of Christ and the Church and the word of the Bible. Augustine's thinking of God moves between the infinitely remote, hidden God, and the God who is manifest and as it were captured by the ecclesiastical intuition of Christ. Whichever way we go with Augustine, we are invariably thrown back upon the other.

In Augustine we find the great breath of the Biblical idea of the one God, in which Christ is not so much as mentioned. But Augustine was also overwhelmed by the idea of Christ, whose corporeal limitation and nearness finally leaves but little room for God.

The memory of Jesus the man, who suffered immeasurably and died the most terrible of deaths, of the man in his lowliness, his humility, and his obedience unto death, is translated into the idea of Christ: The one almighty God assumed the form of a servant for the salvation of men. "His strength is made perfect in weakness," His one immutable reality is fulfilled through death at the hands of this world. Jesus, the man, is a model for us. Jesus, the Christ, the Logos, is God Himself; He saves us if we believe in Him. "He took the form of a servant without losing the form of God, putting on humanity without putting off His godliness, a mediator, insofar as He is a man, and as a man also the way."

The tension between what cannot be reconciled in thought, between the idea of God and the idea of Christ, is not resolved in an insight susceptible of completion, but in Christological and Trinitarian speculations, which are intended not to explain, but to throw light on, the mystery.

The incarnation of God—"to the Greeks foolishness, to the Jews a stumbling block"—contains a sublime meaning to which human reason can gain access: extreme human evil; the profound Jewish conception of suffering; the voice of the Godhead in failure; in the most terrible suffering an intimation of the sacrifice expected of men; a perception not only of man's limitations, but also of the ineradicable remnant of his pride, an error exemplified by all philosophical self-reliance; the humility of the soul that is certain of transcendence. But all this flows from Jesus the man and carries no implication that Jesus is also the Christ, that he is also God Himself.

A. *Philosophical transcending:* In philosophical transcending, Augustine, on Neoplatonic ground, drawing primarily on the passion of his faith in the Biblical One God, develops the following ideas:

Since God is not the object of an immediate perception, knowledge must rise up to Him. In this it is helped by the "proofs of the existence of God." Augustine does not develop them systematically or abstractly, but with a stirring concreteness. "I asked the heavens, the sun, the moon and stars: 'Neither,' say they, 'are we the God whom thou seekest.' I asked the sea and the deeps, and the creeping things that lived, and they replied, 'We are not thy God, seek higher than us.' . . . And I answered unto all these things . . . 'Ye have told me concerning my God, that ye are not He; tell me something about Him.' And with a loud voice they exclaimed, 'He made us.'"

God is everywhere hidden, everywhere manifest. To no one is it given to know that He is, or not to know Him. But atheism, says Augustine, is madness. Heaven and earth and all things proclaim that they are created. Wherein? In the fact that they change and move. "We are, because somebody created us; we did not antecede our own existence, as though we could have made ourselves."

This we know thanks to God. But our knowledge, compared to His, is ignorance. For we do not know God Himself. When we think of God, it is in categories without which no thinking is possible. But since He is subject to no category, we must, thinking of Him in categories, shatter the categories by thinking beyond them. Thus, in Augustine's formulation, we conceive God, if we can, as good without the quality of goodness, as great without quantity, as enthroned above all things but without locality, as encompassing all things but without containing them in Himself, as everywhere but in no definite place, as eternal without time, as Creator of the things that change, but Himself without change.

Though anything we can say is inapplicable, the most appropriate term is "simplicity." For in God no differentiation is possible; neither can substance be differentiated from accident nor subject from predicate. Hence undifferentiated identity, the unity of opposites, are appropriate forms of statement, but they say nothing. The end of thinking about God is silence.

B. *Jesus Christ:* In philosophical transcending, Augustine breaks through all the thinkable. We feel the reality of God by saying nothing. His reality is such that every finite thing and every thought, even the greatest, seems to turn to nothing before Him, and how can God be represented in nothing? If thus, when we try to conceive of God, everything is withdrawn from our finite thinking, so that nothing remains of it, two ways are possible: Either we may accept this utterance of transcending philosophy as an appropriate expression for the existential situation of mortals overpowered by the one reality, or, disillusioned, we may reject it as an indication that for us God is unthinkable and has no being.

Here is the decisive point. Man desires a bodily presence. God is present in Christ. "The word became flesh."

With equal passion Augustine's thinking can do both: it effects the transcending which, because it can contribute nothing to knowledge, ends in silence; and, in the bodily Christ, it accepts the revealed grace of God, who turns to man in the form of His incarnation—for those who are able to believe.

Faith says: God became man. God spoke as a man (though He "might have done everything through the angels"), because it was only in this way that human dignity could be preserved. It "would have been cast away if God had let it appear as though He were unwilling to proclaim His word to man through men."

Christ assumed the "form of a servant" (without losing the form of God) *first* in order to become a model for man. In believing, we discern "what His lowliness can teach us": "in humility we perceive the humble man." The Latin *humilitas* implies: what remains on the ground (*humus*), the lowly, servile, weak, timid; and it implies seeing oneself in all this and so becoming humble (*humilis*). The opposite, pride (*superbia*), is the root of evil in man. Incurable evil is cured by God's self-abasement in assuming the most despised form of humanity. "God has humbled Himself, and man is still proud!"

And, *second*, God became man in order to become an instrument of grace for the redemption of man. Christ died, but through Him death died. "Killed by death, He killed death." For Augustine the two—the example and the grace of the divine act, right human conduct and the vision of divine action—are reflections of one another. And thence result magnificent, absurd propositions which in turn clash to produce new perplexities.

For the suffering and death of Jesus, his crucifixion and resurrection, ascension and entrance into the kingdom of God are at the same time the life of the believer. The perplexities—elucidated by Augustine as abysses of the human condition—are radical. "The Christ who humbled Himself was exalted on the Cross; His abasement could not possibly be anything but grandeur." And correspondingly in man: "Humility is our perfection." The lowest becomes the highest, humility becomes man's glory.

But the forced humility that strives for lowliness and takes delight in it becomes automatically a new pride. Once it is self-satisfied, humility ceases to be humble. In driving myself to humility by asceticism, I show pride; active asceticism, through the power it gains over the self, becomes a triumph of proud selfhood. We find many paradoxes of this kind in Augustine's speculation on freedom and grace.

Let us cast a glance at other consequences of the opposition between *humilitas* and *superbia*:

Augustine demands a conversion of the natural, vital, active, self-assertive attitude—which finds dignity in power and noble bearing and despises base-ness—into a radically opposite attitude that seems impossible in the world.

But in practical reality only a self that has been active and proud can take on a humility that is something more than mere passivity. Only one who self-reliantly ventures in the world can learn that self-reliance does not rest on itself but on that through which I am myself.

Finally: Those whom nature, fortune, and rank have not favored in the world tend to hate the higher, the nobler, the more fortunate. The Christian revaluation, which turns the lower into the higher, becomes a cloak for the revenge of the inferior. A falsification of values gives impotence power, and baseness rank (Nietzsche). These psychological intricacies offer a vast and fertile field for an understanding, discerning psychology.

But all this cannot be turned against the truth at the source of these ideas and realities. For in every reality, in every success, in every triumph, in superiority as such, lies something that is subject to question. There is no joy in victory unless the adversary becomes a friend. Respect for the ad-versary, struggle without hatred, the spirit of conciliation can indeed spring from a sublime will to power, which, as it advances into higher levels of being, always wants still more; but truly and authentically they can spring only from man's awareness of his utter helplessness, of his impotence in the presence of real power, from the humility in which man is never adequate to himself, but seeks the other, seeks all men, for without them he cannot be himself. These considerations are the source of chivalry, of nobility in battle, of solidarity. An unexplored world of the ethos opens up with the mythical idea of Christ, in which the source and model of human action are disclosed in simple signs.

c. *The Trinity:* The idea of God arrived at in philosophical transcending is grounded in reason, while the idea of Christ is grounded in revelation and faith. Philosophical transcending is embodied in operations for which time is a matter of indifference, directed toward the timeless, while the idea of Christ is embodied in a temporally determined, historically decisive faith in a historical event (a mythical faith which distinguishes itself from myth by the historical reality of Jesus the man). The two seem incompatible. From the standpoint of faith, philosophical emotion seems empty; from the standpoint of philosophizing, faith seems absurd. Augustine's conception of the Trinity is intended as a step toward making faith rational, in order that it may be confirmed in philosophizing and that philosophy and faith may become one. Throughout his philosophical life he devoted great effort to these speculations, which he set forth in his compendious work on the Trinity. Yet in this unity of philosophy and faith, which is not a synthesis because in principle Augustine never separates the two, the basic trait of all Augustinian thinking is again disclosed. The Trinity is a mystery of revelation, which in thinking becomes a form of the knowledge of all being and seems to confer the most magnificent insights, but once again ends in the silence of nonknowledge.

For many hundreds of years speculation on the Trinity has enjoyed an extraordinary influence in the Western world. Consequently, though the Trinity is no longer an effective symbol, we may not regard it as a mere absurdity. Let us therefore ask what meanings are manifested in Trinitarian thinking and try to understand the place it held in religious thought.

Here is one motif of Trinitarian speculation: God becomes man in Christ. This is a mystery that can be clarified by the Trinity. The second person, the Logos, becomes man. Without the Trinity, the God-man would be inaccessible to thought. In one of His three persons, the Son or Logos, God becomes man and yet in three persons remains one. Faith-knowledge enhances the mystery: faith still does not understand the incarnation but forms a clearer idea of it.

Another motif of Trinitarian thinking is the striving to penetrate the essence of God: God becomes a person, but He is more than a person. For personality is a human attribute. If God were a person in this sense, He would require other persons with whom to communicate. The impossibility of seeing God as the One absolute person without drawing Him down to the level of human personality leads inevitably to another impossibility, that of thinking God, in His suprapersonality, as a unity of three persons.

The rise and influence of Trinitarian speculation are partly explained by the fact that it discloses the threefold step—dialectic—in all things, in the soul, in every reality. This triple measure in all man's thinking, regardless of its object, is an image of the Godhead. Augustine's triads are almost innumerable. For example: *In the soul:* to be, to know, to live (*esse, intelligere, vivere*); to be, to know, to love (*esse, nosse, diligere*); memory, intelligence, will (*memoria, intelligentia, voluntas*). *In connection with God:* God is the ground of insight, the cause of existence, the order of life (*ratio intelligendi, causa existendi, ordo vivendi*); He is the truth of doctrine, the origin of nature, the happiness of life (*veritas doctrinae, principium naturae, felicitas vitae*). *In all created nature:* permanence, difference, congruence (*in quo res constat, quo discernitur, quo congruit*); to be, to know, to will (*esse, nosse, velle*). *In God Himself:* eternity, truth, will-love (*aeternitas, veritas, voluntas-caritas*).

Since Plato it has been usual to think of the Godhead in threes. Plato had conceived "the being of the good" as a unity of the good, the true, the beautiful (*Symposium*); and another triad embraces God (the Demiurge), the eternal world of Ideas, on which He gazes, and the cosmos of becoming, which He brings forth. Plotinus has the triad of the One who is above being, the realm of Ideas, the world-soul. And, finally, the Christian Trinity: Father, Son-Logos, Pneuma (Holy Spirit).

We may stress the differences: In Plato and Plotinus the Ideas are an independent realm, while in Christian thinking they are the thoughts of God. We may distinguish a triad of the suprasensory (the One, the Ideas, the world-soul, these three Plotinian hypostases—or Father, Logos, Holy Spirit) from a triad that includes the world. We may concentrate on the categories in which the relations among the three persons are conceived (equality, subordination, juxtaposition, interpenetration) and then decide that mere relation is the simplest, the least weighted, and therefore the most appropriate category for the purpose. None of this helps: no mode of thought or representation has any advantage over the others, though some have a peculiar eloquence. All in all we are dealing with permutations and combinations of the concepts and metaphors with which Occidentals have concerned themselves for fifteen hundred years in their efforts to translate the mystery into cognitive knowledge or to fight one another with the *rabies theologorum*. Augustine is a mine where all the possibilities can be found. The task had been set; Augustine took it up and rang the changes on it over and over again. The task was to make the orchestra of ideas play together, to harmonize all the different instruments in the transparent structure of a work; to play the one melody over and over in innumerable modulations, therein to find the logical drama (including the intellectual battles over means and basic tenets) and, finally, to regain the summits of peace in great calm movements that set their seal on the whole.

Augustine never forgets—and he says repeatedly and insistently—that God is unthinkable, ineffable. All thinking and speaking are in vain, but they are indispensable. Thus at the end of his great work (*De Trinitate*), Augustine writes: "I have striven to behold with reason what I believed [*desideravi, intellectu videre, quod credidi*]. . . . There were not many words, because there were only the necessary ones. Save me, O God, from prolixity [*a multiloquio*] . . . I am not silent in my thoughts even if I am silent with my tongue . . . but numerous are my thoughts, that are vain as human thoughts. . . . Grant that I may not consent to them, that even if they should delight me I may reject them." Here we have an outstanding expression of the tension which cannot be overcome in the temporal world and which Augustine experiences in his thinking of God: the striving for knowledge, the passion for thinking, and awareness of the futility of such striving. The authoritative sureness of his assertions is tempered by the way in which from all thought he turns back to God Himself. It is as though Augustine regarded any attempt to encompass God and His innermost thoughts in human representations as an encroachment on God, an importunity. But this is contradicted by the way he brought the whole gamut of available ideas and representations to bear in his unbridled striving to penetrate realms to which no man can attain by thought, though often with an attitude of questioning praise in which a soft note of reticence can be heard.

4. *Philosophical Ideas in the Clarification of Revealed Faith*

The attempt to clarify revealed faith gives rise to philosophical thoughts. If Augustine draws no distinction between philosophizing and the thinking of revealed faith, the question arises: Is a separation possible; that is, can thought retain any truth if the faith in Christ is spent?

A. FREEDOM

A. *Self-reflection:* Constantly scrutinizing his conscience, Augustine discerns impulses, feelings, tendencies that are in conflict with his conscious will. He finds self-deceptions, as, for example, when he prays to God for a sign to justify his postponement of something that should be done at once; when curiosity sets itself up as thirst for knowledge. He recognizes carnal pleasure when, listening to the singing of the Psalter, he finds himself paying more attention to the sound than to the content. He finds it necessary to combat the desire he experiences while eating. He is able to dispense with cohabitation but not with sexual dreams. He likes to do what is right, but in part he does it to make men love him. Always the hidden motive. All human life is perpetual temptation by the senses, by curiosity, by vainglory (the striving to be feared and loved). And we are unaware of it. I cannot know and understand myself. Whatever part of myself I explore, I encounter something I cannot fathom. Augustine inaugurated the psychology that unmasks the soul of man. He observed that there was no end of it and cried out to God: "Greatly I fear my hidden faults that Thine eyes know, but not mine."

B. *The cleavage between will and decision:* Intense self-observation showed him that the will does not will unequivocally. For him the will was the center of existence, life itself. "When I willed or did not will something, I was wholly certain that it was not someone other than I who willed or did not will it." And here, at the center of his being, he experienced a frightening thing (he describes this situation as the state preceding his conversion): "I did not that which with an unequaled desire I longed to do, and which shortly when I should will I should have the power to do. . . . For in such things the power was one with the will, and to will was to do, and yet was it not done; and more readily did the body obey the slightest wish of the soul . . . than the soul obeyed itself."

"Whence is this monstrous thing? and why is it? The mind commands the body, and it obeys forthwith; and mind commands itself, and is resisted." Why? "It wills not entirely; therefore it commands not entirely. . . . For were it entire, it would not even command it to be, because it would already be. It is, therefore, no monstrous thing partly to will, partly to be unwilling, but an infirmity of the mind." The mind is not drawn upward by the truth but downward by habit. "There are two wills." Not two forces, the one good, the other bad, governed him, but rather: "I it was who willed, I it was who was unwilling. . . . I neither willed entirely, nor was I entirely unwilling. Therefore I was at war with myself." The conversion, the leap, came suddenly. At one stroke the gap was bridged. "A light, as it were, of security, was infused into my heart." God had helped him.

Augustine for the first time laid bare without reserve the struggle of the will with itself, the hesitation, the irresoluteness, the significance of the irrevocable decision that engages the whole of life. By his own example he revealed man's weakness. He did not worry about the base and unworthy, but disclosed it as inherent in human nature. But then he laid bare the incomprehensible certainty, the certainty of the will that cannot do otherwise. Will becomes necessity. The fact of willing implies the end of all hesitation, of all uncertainty, of all doubt, but also of all self-constraint. This will is the peace that comes of having chosen and choosing no longer; it is the will that must. The free will cannot do otherwise, that is what makes it free. As long as the will is unfree, it does not truly will and therefore is able to will something else.

What is the freedom of the will that must? Whence does it come? What happens in the decision that brings full and irrevocable certainty of the will?

c. *Dependence and the necessity of a decision:* The finiteness of our existence keeps us in a state of dependence on the world around us, on accidental encounters, on favorable and unfavorable situations. Everywhere, we are dependent on something else. We are in the situation of having to decide (whether to act thus or thus, whether to act or not to act) and of being responsible for our decision.

Augustine explains the certainty of conversion on the basis of two modes of decision. If I have a number of possibilities before me, to test and choose among, will and ability are not the same thing. I decide and act to the best of my ability, but always in respect to particulars. It is otherwise when the decision involves my whole being. Then my will and my ability are the same, but this will comes to me incomprehensibly. I cannot will this will, but through it, because of it, I can will. I do not look on at my decision. I do not bring it about. While deciding, I am already decided. In this decision I do not have myself in hand; I am dependent on God, who gives me to myself.

But if I have thus become aware of my nature as a whole, if then, sacrificing my freedom, I conclude that I am eternally doomed to be thus and cannot become otherwise, Augustine replies: Corruption by original sin is dependent on the grace of redemption and gains hope through faith.

D. *Origin of freedom:* In the freedom of our action, this is the fundamental experience: I will but I cannot will my willing. I must experience the source from which I will. From out of myself I cannot produce this source, this power to decide. I love, but if I do not love, I cannot create love within myself. I am myself, but I can fail myself. I must put my trust in myself, but I cannot rely on myself. A good temperament, an amiable disposition, and other natural traits are not a solid ground. Therefore I am not absolutely free in my will, my freedom, my love. I am given to myself, and thus given to myself I can be free and become myself. In producing myself, I have not produced myself. To myself I owe neither the outward conditions of my existence nor my own self. Hence Augustine says with St. Paul: "What hast thou that thou didst not receive [*quid habes, quid non accepisti*]?"

The paradox remains: It is God who brings forth freedom in man and does not leave him at the mercy of nature. But in so doing God admits the possibility of a human activity against Himself, against God. God leaves man free; but if man turns against God, only God's help and grace can enable him, through his own acts, to turn to the good.

In my freedom for the good I am the work of God. My freedom is freedom that has been given me, not my own. I cannot boast of my freedom. It is pride (*superbia*) to claim credit for what I owe to God. The appropriate attitude is humility in freedom. If I credit myself with what comes from God, I am cast back into my own darkness. It is pride to take pleasure in myself as my own work. Humility is the attitude underlying the truth of all good actions.

E. *The impossibility of being conscious of a good deed:* Augustine knows the perversion of complacency: it is ineradicable, because it is rooted in our very finiteness. In order to act well, I must see the good and recognize my action as good. But such awareness is the beginning of pride. Without knowledge I cannot become good; without knowledge I cannot remain pure. And humility itself, once conscious of itself, is no longer humble but becomes the pride of humility.

The reason for this is man's self-love. He cannot escape from it, except incomprehensibly through the help of God, which enables him to do good without becoming proud, which enables him to experience in the utmost freedom his being given to himself by God. God's help gives him the full freedom with which to attain to God.[2]

F. *Against the Stoics:* Augustine knows their doctrine. Man is free and independent as long as he contents himself with what he can master. He can master only himself, his thoughts and decisions. Consequently, this is all that concerns him. He lives exclusively for himself; he is self-sufficient (autarky). And the Stoic does not doubt that we are indeed master of our own thoughts. He believes we can demonstrate such mastery by guiding our attention and carrying out our resolutions. Our freedom has no ground, but is itself a ground. It is identical with reason. The opposite of freedom is outward constraint. Hence the more independent I am of outside things, and the fewer my needs, the freer I shall be. I remain free if I adapt myself naturally to the world around me. But if, despite my self-sufficiency, I am nevertheless struck by some outward constraint—and such constraints are inevitable in this life—I need not inwardly comply. I become unfree only if I allow my composure to be disturbed. Accordingly, freedom is imperturbable peace of mind (*apatheia*). Through it I remain free even under the most violent constraint from without, even as a slave under torture, even in the most painful sickness. And in extreme cases, I have the freedom to take my life.

In this Stoic attitude Augustine sees nothing but self-deception. Such absence of emotion, such perpetual unconcern would be the death of the soul. Furthermore, such indifference amid pain and constraint is mere imagination. To suppose I have achieved it can only be a delusion. But above all, in the freedom of my decision, it is not through myself that I am free.

G. *Against the Pelagians:* In this last point Augustine opposed Pelagius. For Pelagius man, because created free, is by God's will independent of God. Man has freedom of decision (*libertas arbitrii*). He has the possibility of sinning and of not sinning. Even if he has already decided to sin, there remains a possibility of conversion and hence of freedom. If he wants to, he

---

[2] The great fundamental ideas on the nature of man are universal. This might be shown in a general history of ideas, devoted to the fundamental questions and answers of world philosophy. Here I should merely like to point out an analogy to the sublime ethical attitude just recorded. Chuang-tzu: "No worse thief than virtue and awareness . . . he who considers himself is lost." "The worst is not to get away from oneself." "One does not speak of the great Tao. . . . Great goodness does not set itself up as goodness. . . . The Tao that glitters is not Tao."

can always follow the commandments of God; even after the wickedest life he can always make a new start.

Augustine takes a different view. To his mind, man can do evil by himself, but not good. "The good in me is Thy work and Thy gift, the evil in me is my guilt and Thy judgment." In doing evil the will is free (though not truly free, but free to be unfree); in doing good it needs God. "From the bottom of my heart Thou hast removed the muck of corruption. This means that I no longer will what I will, but will what Thou willst. But where in all these long years was my free will, and from what deep and mysterious hiding place has it now been brought out?" This is Augustine's fundamental experience of the essential transformation effected by his conversion.

H. *Dogmatic formulations:* The conception of God's unfathomable will as the all-encompassing power which also determines man's freedom leads inevitably to the dogma of *predestination.* Each man is predestined to freedom in grace or unfreedom in evil. Man himself cannot change his predestination. No more than he made himself, did he make his freedom. In freedom, he is utterly dependent on God's will, by which his essence is predetermined.

In dogmatic formulations rich in distinctions and complications, fundamental religious conceptions meet and combat one another. We have no need to go into them. But let us briefly indicate the correspondence between the objectivizing schema of Providence in history and the living process at work in the soul of the individual man.

The human condition reflected by this myth sharpened by dogmatic concepts is this: every man is what he is by virtue of historical origin, biological classification, situations he is in or gets into. He is dependent on the equipment given him: memory and brain power, temperament, physical strength. He is dependent on events beyond his control, on the men he sees and speaks with, on the realities he perceives. But in this state of *general dependence,* the individual must perceive the event, the occasion, the reality in order to react to it. Everything he depends on is at once an opportunity he can grasp or let pass, a call he can respond to or not, a language he can understand or not. What I am and what I do is a response. This language remains mute for me if I succumb to mere facticity, to vital impulse, to pleasure and pain, to forgetfulness, to a life of pure momentariness without a horizon and without the Encompassing. It becomes audible and an answer becomes possible if, amid temporal finiteness, there speaks something that Augustine calls God.

The dogmatically elaborated myth is as follows: Original sin—the corrupt state of man and his mortality—is the consequence of the fall of Adam. What was corrupted by Adam is made whole again by Christ. Through him man is reborn. Thus we have a temporal sequence: original condition, fall, inherited sin, redemption. The state of original sin belongs to the world, redemption to transcendence. But while the consequences of original sin endure as long as men are in the world, it is annulled for the believer by the hope of transcendence. These mythical-dogmatic notions reflect the antinomy between the dependence and the freedom of our actual, temporal existence. And on the basis of the myth, the reality of this existence becomes understandable.

The whole process can be framed in a single antithesis: The *world of unfree will* is the ought that the will does not obey, the will that does not fulfill its purpose, the good intentions that are dissipated by lust, the will that cannot will; it is the heeding of the ethical injunction which, though it says: Thou canst because thou shouldst, is actually an inability that cannot recognize itself as such. The *world of free will* opens up when love has no further need of an ought, but accomplishes without good resolutions and dispels the lusts by its reality. This reality can do what it will, because its loving will is itself a being-able.

But man has no choice between the two worlds; in temporality both are in him. One corresponds to his purposive planning; in the other he is given to himself.

1. *The contrast with other types of freedom:* In history we encounter other conceptions of freedom and accordingly other models of personality. By recollecting them, we shall see Augustine more clearly.

There were the *Nordic personalities* who relied on their own strength, who went proudly and unflinchingly to their death, who proved what they were by knowing how to die, and thought of glory. They lived in personal loyalty; they knew gods but were able to defy them, and foresaw the end of the world including the gods.

There were the *Jewish Prophets* who knew themselves to be *instruments of God*. They took upon themselves the obligation to proclaim His word. They refused to be conquered inwardly by the powers of the world, either by their own kings or by the priests, or by the great empires that snatched up the little nations like birds' nests. Only God and the consciousness of obeying God made them free in relation to everything that happened in the world, even toward the hierarchy of the priesthood (historic precursor of the Catholic Church) which claimed to be God's sole representatives on earth. The personality of Western man derived its strength from the contemplation of these Prophets.

There were the many magnificent *Greek personalities,* subordinated to the *idea of measure*; all the natural potentialities of man were embodied in beautiful, and also in immoderate, terrifying personalities.

There was the *Roman personality,* which derived its strength from devotion to the *res publica,* from the sacrifice of the individual. Its thought was pious and purposive, first in the framework of its own people, later identified with the world mission of eternal Rome to ensure the peace and well-being of all men in the imperial order. Though poor in its human embodiments, the Roman personality of the great will exerted an immense influence.

Like nearly all Greek thought, the *Hellenistic personality,* most strikingly in Plotinus, had felt itself to be a link in the cosmos. In his striving to transcend the world and achieve union with the One, Plotinus was merely returning to the world ground. The soul returns home, abandons its worldliness, expands to the infinite, and passes through the hierarchical spheres to merge with the origin. The personality dissolves in speculative mysticism.

These historical manifestations (with the exception of the Nordic and Greek personalities) contain elements of the freedom that went into Augustine's personality. But in Augustine there is something radically different that contrasts with them all. It was Augustine who, though working with heterogeneous, divergent, conflicting ideas, first carried the idea of freedom, which with him loses its beauty, its independence, and its tragic quality, to an unprecedented depth.

This new element springs from Biblical faith and is grounded in St. Paul. But it was not present in Origen or the other early Church Fathers. There may be something of the Prophetic consciousness in it; but the Prophets served God directly, while Augustine served God by way of his belief in the Church. Perhaps Augustine conveyed something of the Roman spirit of self-sacrifice for the benefit of the body politic, but the Romans served the *res publica* and the Imperium, while Augustine served the *civitas Dei,* the Church. Most particularly, Augustine may have taken over some of Plotinus' pure, world-transcending spirituality. But the difference is immense: Augustine was not concerned with the formless One, but with a relation between man and God, between I and Thou. The reality of this fundamental relationship can never be attained in philosophy; but in Augustine it is a great philosophical force. In Augustine man is lifted out of the world more radically than would ever have been possible in cosmic thinking. He stands directly before God. The world is only his dwelling place, what he accomplishes in the world is determined by God. The ancient philosopher remained within this world, though opposing it, standing fast against it as a Stoic, immersing himself in the ground with Plotinus, but in every case alone, only an I, whether asserted or renounced. Augustine, however, stands radically and fundamentally remote from the world, because with God and the spiritual community he sets himself in opposition to it. He does not vanish as a personality in the One, but confronts God and strives toward God; he is himself a personality. He sees his personality as immortal in eternity. If the way in which I experience God is the measure of my own being, then the speculatively conceived, mystically indeterminate One and the personal God of faith must result in very different men. The strangely radiant indeterminateness of Plotinus' selfhood is historically characterized by the disappearance from view of Plotinus the man. He did not wish to be seen, he never spoke of himself. But living a century and a half after Plotinus, Augustine stands before us in the flesh. Here is the personality of a man who dared to bare the ugliest corners of his soul in order to help his fellow believers on their way to God. With him the exploration of the self took on metaphysical depth.

No philosopher before Augustine had concerned himself with the uncertainty of freedom, the ground of its possibility or the question of its actual meaning. But Augustine, thanks to his understanding of St. Paul, considered these matters with an enduring force of conviction.

B. LOVE

A. *The universality of love:* In human life Augustine finds nothing in which there is no love. In everything that he is, man is ultimately will, and the innermost core of will is love. Love is a striving for something I have not (*appetitus*). As weight moves bodies, so love moves souls. They are nothing other than forces of the will (*nihil aliud quam voluntates sunt*). Love is desire (*cupiditas*), where it strives for possession of the beloved; it is joy (*laetitia*), where it possesses; it is fear (*metus*), where it sees its possession threatened and flees the assailant; it is grief (*tristitia*), where it suffers loss. Love is all-encompassing, embracing things and persons, objects of thought and corporeal realities. All these exist for us only if they are not indifferent to us.

Everything a man does, even evil, is caused by love. "Abominations, adulteries, crimes, murders, all offenses—are they not brought about by love?" And to cease loving is no solution. For that is to "be inert, dead, contemptible, wretched." The way out is not to extinguish a dangerous love, but to purify it: "Guide toward the garden the water that is flowing into the sewer." "Love, but take heed what you love." "Love what is worthy of love."

B. *True love:* Worthy of love is that beyond which we can find nothing better. That is God. All true love is love of God. And to God we attain only through love. What is loved in the love of God? The permanent and unchanging, the life that does not die, the good that can and should be loved, not for the sake of something else but for itself; that in the possession of which all fear of losing it ceases, so that there is never grief over its loss and the joy of possession is indestructible.

But all this is put negatively. The highest good itself is not expressed, but designated as that from which fear, care, uncertainty, loss, and death in the world are absent. All the dangers of love in the world have vanished. Are the contents of our love in the world preserved, freed from their deficiencies and confirmed from another source? Or if not, what is the positive element in what we love as God?

It is uttered only in effusive, identical propositions, not in terms of something else: to love God is to love Him gratuitously (*gratis*) and not to seek a reward apart from God. "Beseech Him for thy salvation; and He will be thy salvation; beseech not salvation from elsewhere." And consequently: "What were everything Thou gavest me, apart from Thee! That is to say: love God gratuitously: hope to receive God from God; hasten to be filled with God, sated by God. For He will suffice thee; beside Him nothing can suffice thee."

The love of God is unique, in this world and for all eternity. Faith and hope belong to this existence in time; but love remains: "For even if a man has attained to eternal life and the other two virtues have ceased, love [that is, the love of God] will still be present, in increased degree and with greater certainty."

c. *Love determines the nature of man:* A man's essence is in his love. "To ask whether a man is good, is not to ask what he believes or hopes, but what he loves." "A good man is not one who knows what is good, but one who loves what is good."

Where there is love of God, love has an object on which it can rely. The man who is filled with it will everywhere see the good and do what is right. To him it may be said: Love and do what thou wilt (*dilige et, quod vis, fac*). For he who sees God becomes so small in his love of Him that he prefers God to himself not only in judgment but in love itself. Here it becomes impossible to sin. From this love man cannot backslide into self-complacency.

Once discerned, this great good "is so easily attained, that the will is the possession of what is willed." For nothing is so easy for the good will as to have itself, to have what it wills.

D. *The modes of love:* We are in the world. God is not visible but only present for faith. Our love which in the present desires its object is manifold, directed at objects in the world, and consequently not a pure love of God. The fundamental distinction in our loving lies therefore in the direction of movement, either toward God (*caritas*) or toward the world (*cupiditas*).

Caritas, the love of God (*amor Dei*), loves what alone can be loved for its own sake, and loves everything else for the sake of God. *Cupiditas,* love of the world (*amor mundi*), strives for temporal things. Without relation to God, this love is perverse, it is called *libido*; it is love of the flesh (*carnalis cupiditas*).

Either the movement of love is toward an object of desire that I have not, or else I have arrived at my goal and am in possession of it. On the way, I love something for the sake of something else; at the goal, I love it for itself. On the way, I can use (*uti*) something for the sake of something else; at the goal I can enjoy (*frui*) it for itself.

But since only God is worthy to be loved for Himself and the only true love is the love of God, the *frui* is justified only in connection with God, while in connection with earthly things only an *uti* is in order. Thus the essence of all perversion of love is to use what should be enjoyed and enjoy what should be used. In other words: love for people and things in the world is true only if they are loved for the sake of God, not for their own sake. And the worst perversion of all would be to make use of God in order to enjoy people and things in the world.

E. *The order of love* (ordo amoris): We are in the world and it is as beings in the world that we love. If love of God and worldly love were entirely separate, they would exclude one another. But worldly love is forbidden only when it is a *frui* rather than an *uti,* that is, when any being other than God is loved wholly for his or its own sake. It is in such cases, says Augustine, that the soul is sullied by love of the world.

Thus the essential is an order of love (*virtus et ordo amoris*) in which the love of God and worldly love are combined in the right way. This order implies that *uti* and *frui* must not be confused, that all things in the world should be loved only in the sense of an *uti,* not enjoyed for their own sake. It turns out, however, "that God, even here in the world, gives us goods which are desirable for their own sake," such as wisdom, friendship, while others are necessary for the sake of something else, such as doctrine, food, drink. We cannot do otherwise: This *frui* is *cum delectatione uti,* an *uti* with enjoyment. When the object of love is present, it necessarily brings joy with it. In the *Retractationes,* Augustine explicitly modifies his original judgment: He had said that to love the visible body was alienation from God. But it is no alienation from God to love corporeal forms in praise of God.

Or stated differently: All things in the world are worthy of love: "As with the beauty of the body, so it is with every creature. Insofar as it is good, it can be loved in a good or evil way, in a good way if the order is observed; in an evil way if it is reversed." Augustine even thought it permissible to love one's own body. "No one hates his body." To love something more than the body does not mean to hate the body.

Augustine employs the parable of the *wayfarer* to indicate what love in the world means; to show how, because of its drive to go farther, it can yield satisfaction but not fulfillment. Loved ones shelter us when we are weary and needful of rest; they refresh us, but then they send us on our way toward God, who alone is lasting peace. The foot rests when the wayfarer lies down; this gives his will a respite and provides a certain well-being, but that is not what he is striving for. The resting place is a source of true satisfaction only if it is looked upon as a night lodging, not as a home. To rest among friends profits the wayfarer's movement toward the eternal.

F. *The love of God, of self, of our fellow men:* Self-love and love of our fellow men have their place in worldly love ordered by the love of God.

Self-love is right and necessary. It is not possible that a man who loves

God should not love himself. Moreover, one whom God loves loves himself, but he who loves God more than himself loves himself in the right way.

According to Augustine, love of our fellow men is next in importance after self-love. For who is closer to man than man? We are all descended from Adam and are related by lineage. Revelation speaks to us all through Christ, and we are one in faith.

But if love of our neighbors, our fellow men, is to be true love, it must take the form of *caritas*, not of *cupiditas*. *Caritas* is the bright, serene love of one soul for another (*serenitas dilectionis*); *cupiditas* is the tumultuous night of instinct (*caligo libidinis*).

Love is reciprocal. The lover "burns the more ardently the more he sees the other soul seized by the same fire." There is "no stronger power to awaken and increase love than to see oneself loved if one did not love, or to hope to be loved in return if one was the first to love." Love always strives to bind two together. From general benevolence, it becomes friendship (*amicitia*): "I felt that my soul and the soul of my friend had become one soul in two bodies."

These are rare sentences in Augustine. Christian-Augustinian love is directed wholly toward one's neighbor, toward every neighbor as a man. Man is not loved as an individual. God loves the man whose love is reflected in self-love. Love of my fellow men spurs me and guides me to the love of God. It includes the sinner and my enemy. "For in him thou lovest not what he is, but what thou wishest him to be" (*non quod est, sed quod vis, ut sit*), namely his love of God that makes him lovable.

G. *Characterization:* In the history of the philosophy of love (Plato, Dante, Bruno, Spinoza, Kierkegaard) Augustine's thinking takes an essential place. Like all philosophy of love, he taps the source that is essential to man, the absolute, unrestricted, transcendent on which all fullness and meaning depend, by which everything is measured.

In Augustine's *caritas* three elements converge: the perfection of an acosmistic feeling of love; the having (*frui*) that no longer desires; active help and succor. All this is impersonal, it can be accomplished in the human community, the *corpus mysticum* of Christ. To love God implies: awareness of eternity, through which and in which everything is—not mere confidence in being, but a conscious affirmation of being as being—a happiness without object.

Certain critical questions may be asked: (1) Is this a fundamental awareness of the fullness of being or is it an escape from hopeless misery to an exaltation and intensification of the self? (For does not Augustine say that our greatest peace here below is "not so much joy in happiness as consolation in unhappiness"?) (2) Does real love in the world tend in Augustine to transform itself into an extramundane love that is consequently unreal in the world? Is the love which is possible in the world, which in historic form can cut across time to become an eternal present, neglected in favor of an unhistorical, universal, impersonal, abysmally lonely love, which knows only God and knows Him only in the Church and the revelation guaranteed by the Church? (3) Are these two questions grounded in a theme to be found in all Augustine's thinking, a theme which transforms the possible momentary experience of eternity into something situated in the future, in another world, a kind of future time transcending time? And is this, rather than the philosophical proposition that the reward of a good action is the action itself, a source of the dissociation of ethical action from ensuing reward or punishment? Does this mean that world and other world are divided into two realities?

These questions are hard to answer in relation to Augustine. From him come impulses that we regard as true, but often a clear sign degenerates into opaque objectivity and the result is a perpetual narrowing. Such conceptions of future and other world can be true—they need not be materialized into reality or result in the separations of which we have been speaking. But, on the other hand, such degeneration can easily take place.

C. WORLD HISTORY

A. *Augustine's schema and its consequences:* The history of mankind is the story of Creation and man's original estate, of Adam's fall and the original sin that came with it, of the incarnation of God and the redemption of man. Now we are living in a period of indeterminate duration, to be concluded by the end of the world, after which there will remain only hell and the kingdom of heaven.

The intervening history is essentially of no importance. All that matters is the salvation of every soul. But the great realities of the Roman state and the Catholic Church are present. After the conquest of Rome by Alaric (410), the pagans blamed the Christians for the catastrophe. Because they have forsaken the old gods, the gods have forsaken Rome. Augustine undertook to vindicate them in his great work, *The City of God,* in which a view of history plays an important part. From the beginning, since Cain and Abel, there have been two states, the worldly state (*civitas terrena*), which goes back to Cain and sin, and the divine state (*civitas Dei*), which goes back to Abel and his life that was pleasing to God. Since Christ these states have been manifest.

All human existence is twofold. The fall of Adam ushered in a society based on natural reproduction, in which men are dependent on one another and have combated one another since Cain. Men form communities that wage war. They organize the sinful life. Yet at the same time each individual exists as a creature of God, in an immediate relation to God. These individuals gather together in the community of faith. They encourage one another to lead the true life according to the will of God; however, in so doing they depend not on each other but only on God, that is, on revelation and the Church.

For Augustine the concrete consequences of these two aspects of human existence were Church and state, the Catholic Church and the Roman Empire. All history was a struggle between the divine state and the worldly state.

B. *Augustine's range of interest. His method of proof and interpretation:* Augustine answers all historical questions with arguments drawn not from an empirical investigation, but from revelation. Thus the duration of the world is 6,000 years since the creation of Adam. This we know from the Bible. The essential is that man and world have not always existed. The brevity of the time that has elapsed since the Creation does not, in Augustine's opinion, detract from the credibility of the schema, and moreover it is a matter of no importance. For even if many, many thousands of years had elapsed, over against infinity any enumerable period of time would be like a drop of water beside the ocean.

In seeking to explain why any particular historical event occurred, Augustine declares that human knowledge cannot fathom God's purposes: God confers the Empire on Augustus and Nero alike, on Constantine the Christian and Julian the Apostate. Or else he suggests possible interpretations: Constantine was granted great success as a Christian ruler as a demonstration to men that the worship of pagan gods was not necessary for a brilliant rule; other Christian rulers were unsuccessful, lest Christianity be regarded as a safeguard against earthly failure. Nevertheless, it is the greatest good fortune for mankind if a truly pious ruler also possesses the art of governing his nation. Or another interpretation: The world dominion of the Romans was their deserved reward for their love of freedom and striving for glory, though these were the pagan virtues of men who knew no higher realm than their earthly fatherland. Furthermore, the Empire was an example by which Christians might learn how to love their heavenly fatherland and incur great sacrifices for its sake.

The study of political history is held to be meaningless, since faith knows that God's will is responsible for everything we do not understand. The events of the secular Empire are said to merit no interest but are judged nevertheless. Empires, when justice is absent, are nothing more than great robber bands, just as bands of robbers, when they grow strong, are empires. "The Roman Empire grew by injustice alone. It would have been small if its neighbors had been peaceful and righteous and had not provoked war by their wrongdoing. Then, for the happiness of the world, all countries would be small and live in neighborly harmony." As we see, Augustine accepts the Roman theory that the wars of Rome were just, that the injustice was with the others.

However, following the analogy of the six days of Creation, Augustine sees the structure of history in the sequence of epochs marking the progress of the kingdom of God in the world: from Adam to the Flood, from the Flood to Abraham, from Abraham to David, from David to the Babylonian captivity, from the Babylonian captivity to Christ, from Christ to the end of the world. With his meager insight into political trends, he did not regard Alaric's conquest of Rome as final. Rome had survived many catastrophes and would no doubt outlive this one.

His general view of history is never based on investigation but solely and explicitly on Biblical revelation. A modern reader notes, however, that it also reflects Augustine's own experience: his personal conversion and its consequences. The events of the individual are those of the world, and conversely. Events of long duration are at the same time immediately present. The great Christian thinkers saw their own history as one with Christian history.

c. *Historicity:* This belief made possible for the first time an essentially historical view of human existence (in contrast to the purely cyclical existence of nature). For now the past is binding and makes man what he is. But the essence of the human past is sin, which makes political life necessary and valid. But, paradoxically, it is the sinful past that must be wholly transcended and eradicated along with political life. This comes about through the divine state, the City of God, where, thanks to the revelation of Christ, the individuals making up the community of faith first perceive the historical fact that is to be transcended. Because the individual as a creature lives in a bond with God, but can only achieve the true bond through historical revelation, he is aware that as a man he must live historically amid the sinfulness inaugurated by the fall of man and enduring even after the incarnation, and will be saved through his faith in the incarnation, an event that occurred at a definite historical time. Both states are historically grounded, one in the fall of man, the other in revelation. What was hidden from the beginning was made manifest with Christ.

Apart from the two states, the dual historic character of man has other consequences: the two modes of love—on the one hand the love of God, on the other, world love and self-love—and the two modes of human equality, the one rooted in a common faith and the other in a common, sinful past.

D. *Characterization of Augustine's philosophy of history:* Augustine has been regarded as the founder of the Western philosophy of history. And indeed it was he who first clearly formulated the question of the whence and whither of history. He aroused an awareness of the transcendentally grounded historicity of man. He expressed this insight in its specifically Christian form: he saw the limited, temporal character of Church and state and formulated the struggle between them. He interpreted the tension of all human existence between true faith and false unbelief on the basis of its historical manifestation.

But it did not so much as occur to Augustine to base his schema of history on an investigation of the facts. The philosophically grounded universal histories of recent centuries sprang from a different source and cannot be regarded as "secularizations" of Augustine's views. Their fundamental attitude is that of modern science: to investigate the empirical world and so discover facts and limits which philosophy interprets. The new view of history thus developed has vastly broadened and critically secured our empirical knowledge of history, and it is still advancing over paths whose end is not in sight. But the speculative schemata have lost their restrictive power. For example, such alternatives as cycles of eternal return or unique linear history have lost their cogency. Since the pretension to total knowledge—whether metaphysical or scientific—has been abandoned, such alternatives have been replaced by two kinds of method:

What they contain of cosmologically ascertainable fact is a question of investigation, and to investigation as such there is no end. In respect to particular phenomena, linear uniqueness and cyclic recurrence are hypotheses to be examined and verified. As a whole, they are without relevance for human knowledge, which knows no limits in its advance and keeps discovering new perspectives that lead beyond all seemingly conclusive generalizations.

What they signify as *symbols* relates to man and his possible *Existenz*. Here both conceptions, the single line and the recurrent cycle, have possible meaning for one and the same *Existenz* in different contexts; the line for the earnestness of the eternal decision, the circle for the earnestness of eternal actuality in repetition. In the existential situation the battle of the symbols begins when an attempt is made to claim absolute validity for them in the wrong place, that is, in a context where they lead to nothing. It does not spring from any conclusive universal knowledge that is compelled on theoretical grounds to decide for one or the other. Such a total decision is as meaningless philosophically as it is scientifically impossible. It denotes an inept, empty form of rationalistic philosophy that delights in pseudoscientific argumentation. Argumentation of this sort may have been more justified at a time when consciousness as a whole had not yet been illumined by the universally scientific attitude of our day and when the authentic philosophical impulses had not yet been reawakened.

IV. CHARACTERIZATION AND CRITIQUE

1. *The Personality in Its First General Aspect*

Augustine's personality, though it stands before us almost in the flesh, is a riddle. This always active mind, driven by impetuous passion, encompassing all the knowledge of his time, perpetually elucidates itself and communicates its self-exploration in a striving for perfect openness. Yet in the end we are left questioning. His nature seems to disclose noble and commonplace traits. His thinking moves in the most sublime speculations and in rationalistic platitudes; it is sustained by lofty Biblical ideas of God and succumbs not infrequently to superstition. The great questions he treats are forces in his own life. He seems bold and venturesome and yet remains anchored, almost without danger, in his unfailing fundamental certainty. His thinking moves in vast contradictions. It is always related to his actual experience and at the same time to the One on which everything depends; it is addressed to the adversaries that happen to come along, and attuned to practical tasks. By creating many works in response to changing situations, it produced an "opus," which he rightly conceived as a coherent whole and which has been an object of interpretation for fifteen hundred years.

2. Comparison with Kierkegaard and Nietzsche

For us of the present day a comparison with Kierkegaard and Nietzsche is illuminating. All three were moved by deep, original emotion. They thought passionately, eruptively, from out of their experience of being-human. They underwent radical transformations and wrote unremittingly. The immediacy of their thinking seems to hover over the groundlessness of their personal being; they do not crystallize into a personality but appear in many personalities. They all think by penetrating to the fundamental, with a psychology that is an elucidation of *Existenz,* with doctrines that have their function in the vitality of their operations of thought. They write with their blood. Hence what is so inimitable and so provocative in much of what they say. They accept the risk of contradiction because they evade no authentic impulse, but follow each one, impelled by their drive toward the whole, comprehensive truth. Their thinking with its many contradictory possibilities is like life itself. Yet they think with an intensity that is always systematic though the system is never completed. All three have a creative attitude toward language that is unintentional though they reflect on it afterward. The rhetorical prolixity of Augustine, the stylistic mannerisms of Nietzsche are the surface aspects of this joy in speaking. All three have a maximum of conscious self-understanding and self-control. Augustine wrote the first true autobiography and (like Kierkegaard and Nietzsche) concluded his written work with a critical retrospect. They give the reader not a mere content but an interpretation of it, a reflection on its meaning. Because in all three the content took on a personal aspect, the philosopher's self-portraiture became a part of it.

All these analogies bear witness to the depth of Augustine's emotion, his capacity for extreme experience, the power of his personality, his "modernity." But they are overshadowed by a radical difference: Augustine's lifelong determination to participate in the building of a community, his worldly wisdom, his untiring practical activity. In all his writings, the mood is different from that of the Great Awakeners: his passion was accompanied by a sense of measure and responsibility. For Augustine speaks in the name, and under the authority, of the Christian community of faith, the Church. The freedom with which he did so was possible only at that moment of Church development. Kierkegaard and Nietzsche were solitary individuals, exceptions, and they knew it. Augustine was a founder; loyal subject of a world power, he served the Church. All his thoughts were anchored in a single truth, and he himself entered into a tradition secured by authority. Kierkegaard stood in solitary opposition to the Church, a police spy in the service of God, as he put it. Nietzsche was a lone individual, without a God, boundlessly questioning and questionable, vainly seeking a support in "eternal return," "will to power," "Dionysiac life." Augustine's loneliness, though unrelieved in human terms, was overcome by his membership in the Church.

3. *Ecclesiastical Thinking*

A. Augustine's greatness and limitation lie in the originality of his conception of ecclesiastical authority. Dissatisfaction with philosophy made him a Christian, obedient to the authority of the Church: "I should lend no credence to the Gospel if the authority of the Catholic Church did not impel me to do so."

Perhaps it will be asked whether Augustine was a philosopher or a theologian. In regard to a man of Augustine's day, the distinction is not yet applicable. He was both in one, not one without the other. He knew that his thinking was free only by virtue of his faith in divine revelation. For him there was no *a priori* antagonism between authority and reason, faith and knowledge.

In Augustine's experience free philosophy was empty and conferred no happiness. He abandoned it in favor of revealed faith, whose meaning and blessing he conceived to be embodied in theological dogma. But for Augustine, unlike later dogmatists, theology was still in process of development. He did not deduce his ideas from dogmatic principles. For he was still faced with the task of elaborating the dogmatic contents of faith, of developing the unclear sources into a definite faith. His thinking is often independent, philosophical, original, though moving in the area and atmosphere of revealed faith. It is a thinking that penetrates and makes for awareness. It is philosophy.

As a Christian, Augustine became a philosopher who interpreted the Church and the Bible. He did not forsake reason but used it to build up a knowledge rooted in faith. With him the authoritarian thinking which we are bound to regard as opposed to philosophy, becomes philosophical, that is to say, original. His attitude raises questions that are still alive today, only seemingly solved. Even when philosophy opposes this attitude, even when it rests on a faith that has nothing to do with revelation or the Church, it should do everything in its power to understand this other faith.

B. For Augustine the authority of the Church was supreme because initiated by the Creator of all things in His revelation. It was also a source of security in the most reliable of communities, based not on human contract but on God's incarnation. For this reason all men belong to it. The proof of its truth is that it embraces the whole world from Spain to the Orient (the ancient idea of a *consensus gentium*); such heretics as the Donatists were a purely local phenomenon. Only folly or stubborn malice could reject the claim of catholicity, for which reason it was permissible to reinforce proof with universal coercion. This proof of catholicity has been historically refuted. But even today there remains a vestige of it in the sense of community that animates the Catholic believer, that enables him to regard his Church and his cult as a home in every part of the earth.

It must never be forgotten that all Augustine's ideas are grounded in his unshakable confidence in the authority of the Church, which alone leads to Christ and through Him alone in turn to God. Augustine gave magnificent expression to propositions and movements of thought embodying a fundamental self-certainty and certainty of God. But after his conversion, it would not have occurred to him to philosophize in existential independence, before God alone—without mediator and without the Church. He was sheltered; it was no longer possible for him to despair, to suspect that God is not, or that He is a being against whom the soul rebels in crime and madness because of its unbearable and undeserved sufferings. Augustine is not just a man with whom we as men can enter into free communication—communication with him presupposes recognition of the authority he recognized; it presupposes those "other witnesses" of the common faith. His philosophical thinking culminates in dogmatic thinking, and both are justified only in Church thinking.

It would be a mistake to measure Augustine by the standard of heretics, sectarians, Protestants, who dared to defy the authority of the Church on the basis of a higher (and usually exclusive) authority revealed to them directly by the Bible, and on this basis to accuse him of lack of courage. He showed plenty of courage in the course of his life. He himself built up his faith in authority; it was not forced on him. He was not born into it, but acquired it through conversion, and then grew into it. It was not habit but his own positive truth that brought him fulfillment. Defiance of the Church would have been self-destruction for Augustine. To renounce it was so impossible that it could not even have been regarded as a temptation. He never came into conflict with Church authority, for he himself was one of its spiritual creators. The Church was above any antagonism that might have resulted in a conflict. And Augustine situated even his most radical thoughts in the sphere of the Church.

Indeed, he shows no trace of the ancient philosophers' tendency to independence. He needed and desired something other, something coming from outside, to which he could hold. This other, the Church, is so powerful in Augustine because he did not find it ready-made, but helped with his thinking to construct it. It was his freedom that supplied the movement of truth in this thinking.

c. Both *ecclesiastical faith and philosophical faith* profess their nonknowledge. Through it *ecclesiastical faith* adheres, amid all contradictions, to the reality of the Church as corporeal presence, and through it philosophical faith holds fast to the utterly hidden God, who speaks an ambiguous language in the world and whose very existence is doubtful. *Philosophical faith* stands in the concreteness of its always unique, noncatholic, historical actuality, through which it is able to ascertain the true reality, for which there is no guarantee except in the freedom of man and its communicative realization on the brink of the abyss of failure in the reality of the world.

Nonknowledge finds its ecclesiastical fulfillment in the concrete existence and many manifestations of the one Church, and its philosophical fulfillment in the venture of its existential historicity, springing from many converging sources, drawn toward an absolutely transcendent One that has no universally valid embodiment.

Augustine had taken the step from a materialistic, Manichaean, skeptical attitude to the transcendent spirituality of Plotinus, the reality of the spiritual as such. But his nature demanded something tangible even in transcendent reality. A life in the uncertainty of nonknowledge drove him to despair. He did not wish to seek without finding. And he was not satisfied to forget the corporeal and live in the pure spirit. The spirit itself had to take on body. This it did through the authority of the Church and through the Church in Christ, the incarnate God.

Hitherto all philosophy had addressed itself to an obscure and unorganized world of individuals. Political philosophy had been the quest for a state in which individuals might thrive. Augustine was the greatest of those who wished to think for all, to take responsibility for the thought and practical action of the whole community.

In this striving for "catholicity," was philosophy renouncing itself or rising to new heights? In Augustine we find no sign of intellectual suicide. He looked upon no thought as forbidden and surely a *sacrificium intellectus* was not in his intention. But he did not bring about catholicity in men's thinking. What he regarded as "catholic" has split historically into many churches, all of which together encompass only a fraction of mankind.

D. By his philosophy Augustine contributed appreciably to three characteristics of the Church: its *power,* its *methods of thought,* its *magic.*

(1) He believed that God's sovereignty as embodied in space and time should be unlimited. Paradoxically, an experience of man's helplessness gave

rise to what for a thousand years was to be the mightiest *organization of human power,* an organization which condemned any independent impulse as rebellion against God. At the same time, it opened wide its arms to embrace all who, regardless of their particular nature or institutions, professed allegiance to it.

Augustine was part and parcel of the vast spiritual and political development of this institution that dominated the Western world until the beginning of the modern era. And in this development the inwardness of the beginnings was astoundingly reversed: Contempt for the world became domination of the world; contemplation became an undeviating will; freedom through profound reflection became union through coercion; the knowledge and speculation grounded in nonknowledge became a body of doctrine; the temporal movement of searching became the world of dogma, immutable, subject to no doubt, no longer an object of penetrating thought but a presupposition.

Self-submission engendered a tendency to repression; self-sacrifice led men to demand the same sacrifice of others. And the enduring uncertainty (for certainty would have required among other things a universal acceptance of the faith) made it intolerable to witness the existence of others for whom the Church was not even an enemy but solely a matter of indifference. All this, added to a sense of power, intensified the claim of catholicity, the demands "upon all."

It has been said that this ecclesiastical thinking represents a fusion of Christianity with the Roman spirit of Empire, of world organization and law. The pagans believed the Roman Empire to be eternal, and even the Christians thought it might well endure as long as the world itself. This eternity of the Empire, it is held, was reflected in the eternity of the Catholic, ecumenical Church. But the comparison should not be carried too far. The Roman Empire was remarkably tolerant toward all forms of custom and belief (with the sole exception of the Christian faith, which it condemned for its intolerance). The Church vastly enhanced its concept of authority, which it extended to the innermost soul through its claim to be the sole mouthpiece of God. As Augustine saw it, this meant that the state itself was under obligation to help the Church enforce its demands.

(2) This Church aspired to be all things to all men, to be catholic. Whatever is humanly possible must have its justification and at the same time its order and hence limitation. From the outset this was implicit in the spirit of ecclesiastical thinking. In practice, this means that everything has its place: the ascetic monk and the emperor who rules the world, celibacy and marriage, contemplation and worldly activity. Theoretically, it gives rise to an impressive intellectual edifice, a *complexio oppositorum,* which is suitable for world conquest because everything can find a place in it, and is radical in only one point: the absolute claim of Church authority. But this general form of ecclesiastical thinking cannot be identified with the specific thinking

of Augustine. Augustine's thinking is far too passionate to strive for the tranquillity of systematic total knowledge, far too much interested in the particular to perceive the totality otherwise than in God's unfathomable unity and in the universal love of God. But in his many systematic operations and in the actual contradiction that extends to every sphere of his thinking, Augustine gave ecclesiastical thinking its most valuable and effective tools.

(3) If the Church is to embrace all men, its *corporeal manifestations* must meet all needs. By his ecclesiastical thinking, Augustine increased the currency of superstition. With his doctrine that the sacrament of baptism gives even the newborn babe purification, rebirth, and eternal bliss (which are denied the child who dies unbaptized), he promoted the *magical* conception of the sacrament.

E. Along with its world renunciation, the model of life provided by Augustine signified a striving to show all men the way to eternal salvation, to work for them as a priest, and through the authority of the Church to rule over them. Augustine said yes to the world—at the end of the Creation, God saw that it was good—but never to the point of experiencing worldly actuality, even the worldly actuality illumined by transcendence, as a fulfillment (except for the things of the Church); he never went so far as to develop an inner-worldly ethos springing from the realities in this world. He saw the virtues of the Romans, their spirit of sacrifice and thirst for glory in devotion to the state, but these remained beyond the pale of beatitude. He did not see or know human warmth and loyalty, human love and friendship. For him the individual was replaceable, not before God, but for other men. Community existed only in faith or the duty of mutual aid. Each man is utterly alone, because he is himself only through God and with God, not with and through another human self. Loneliness is overcome not by communication, but through God. Self-love comes before love of others.

Communication itself becomes subject to the conditions of authority. In an early work, Augustine expresses his desire to convince rather than to command. When he spoke with the Manichaeans, he insisted that, if the dialogue were to have any meaning, neither party must claim to be in definitive possession of the truth. But nothing remained of these intimations of another possibility.

F. In the reality of Augustine and the Church there lies an immense question. For through them the *striving for the truth which binds and brings peace* is not only attested but also perverted. The great striving is attested by imposing figures: Augustine created the area of thought in which Gregory the Great, Anselm, and Thomas Aquinas became possible. It was perverted, because it brought more violent, more ruthless, and more treacherous struggles into the world than there had ever been before; because the claim to sole possession of the truth, that is, the one valid revelation of the One God, led within Christendom to fanatical, self-destructive conflict among the "denominations" and, on the outside, to wars of conquest, the Crusades. Every lust for power was justified as standing in the service of God. This is not the place to describe what followed. But it is perhaps the strangest note in our Western history that so much depth in the exploration of every humanly possible question, so much noble humanity, so much authentic piety should have been so closely allied with the evil forces they were striving to combat.

An outsider can never fully understand the reality of true ecclesiastical faith. Of course we can see the outward phenomenon. We see the structures, the methods of exerting power, from the sublime forms that overwhelm the soul to the crude forms that the political power of the Church has often taken. We do not see what the religious martyr experiences in death, alone with God. Psychologically, such experience is as inaccessible to us as the enthusiastic obedience, the self-sacrifice and death of so many Communists. We confront a power that breaks off communication, withdraws into itself, speaks always on the assumption that it alone possesses the one truth, and in decisive moments employs the force which it otherwise humbly condemns, sometimes to the point of exterminating whole peoples and cultures in God's name (the Albigensian Crusade), of loving its enemies by massacring them.

G. Where Augustine deals with the eternal questions of philosophy, it seems to me that I am witnessing movements of philosophical thought. Yet nowhere else have I so provocative, so alarming an impression of seeing a movement of philosophical thinking flow from an antiphilosophical principle inherent in Christian ecclesiasticism. Augustine teaches us to see the reality of ecclesiasticism even from our remote vantage point by the way in which he and his philosophizing move within it.

4. *Contradictions in Augustine*

First some examples of grave contradictions:

A. *The source of evil:* Augustine rejected the two primordial powers of the Manichaeans. For God is one. But what then is the source of evil?

Evil is nothing. Because man is made out of nothing, he is sinful. But this nothing that can have no influence (for if it could, it would be something) becomes at once a stupendous power. *Nothing* stands opposed to God.

Evil is man's freedom, which through the fall of Adam and the resultant original sin turns against God in every man. It is not God who brings about evil, but man. But God has permitted it.

God is immutable and this implies that evil is not. But the overwhelming reality of evil compels us to recognize its existence and try to explain its origin. According to the situation, Augustine took now one, now the other of these positions. The contradiction is evident.

In interminable discussions, men have tried to sharpen and clarify this contradiction: on the one hand, evil is a mere clouding of the good, a shadow, a deficiency; on the other hand, it is an enormously effective power. But no one has succeeded in resolving it. Various arguments have been brought forth: Granted, evil in itself is nothing, but it is not nonexistent. It is nothing because no divine Idea corresponds to it. But since evil is done, it is not nonexistent. Because Augustine saw evil as the consequence of an original act—the fall of Adam—his doctrine implied not a metaphysical, substantial dualism like that of the Manichaeans, but an ethical dualism, which came into the world through God-given freedom and would cease with the end of the world and the last judgment. But say others, God created a freedom that could turn against Himself; thus He Himself is indirectly the author of evil; and the division between the two realms will endure even after God's last judgment. In this view a modified form of Manichaean-Iranian dualism—here light, there darkness—found its way into Christian dogma after all.

Dualism runs through the whole of Augustine's work and takes various forms: God-world, *civitas Dei–civitas terrena,* belief-unbelief, *caritas-cupiditas,* sin-grace.

B. Augustine's attitude *toward the world* involves a radical contradiction. The world is God's creation, it is good, it is beautiful as a work of art, the disharmonies increase its beauty. Even evil is in general an element in the good. Without the fall of Adam, we should not have the glory of the Saviour, the God who became man. But on the other hand: It is the highest wisdom to despise the world and strive for the kingdom of heaven—which transcends all temporality. For here below, as we have heard, our only peace is consolation in misery.

C. The *Church* is the kingdom of heaven, "we are its citizens," "all the good faithful are elect." The *civitas Dei* is the congregation of the faithful, that is, of the saints. But the Church as it actually is includes non-saints and even unbelievers. Thus Augustine conceives of an invisible, true Church in contrast to the visible Church. It becomes possible to conceive of saints, members of the City of God, living outside the Church.

The distinction between the two Churches is sharpened by the idea of predestination. In the freedom of His unfathomable decision God elected some to live in a state of grace, others to serve as vessels of His wrath. He permits some of the elect to live outside the visible Church, and others who have been condemned forever to live within it. By God's will the elect who dwell in the invisible Church are immutably what they are. They have no need of the visible Church. But the visible Church (and with it Augustine) maintains that all men are dependent on the instruments of grace (sacraments) of this same visible Church. "Outside the Church there is no salvation," and here again Augustine means the visible Church. At the end of all these contradictions stands an unshakable faith in the Church: the Church is real, yet beyond our understanding.

This rational contradiction in Augustine corresponds to an inner tension that is expressible only as contradiction: In ecclesiastical thinking he found complete certainty; the authority of the Church sheltered him and sustained him, gave him peace and happiness. But in reflecting on God's eternal, inscrutable decision, the immutable predestination of every individual either to grace or damnation, he is assailed by uncertainty. No one, he says, can know to what he is predestined. It might seem as though Augustine did not fully rely on the guarantees of the Church. He seems to shift back and forth between the uncertainty of election and the certainty bestowed by membership in the Church. What remains is the unrest of a man who wishes to become neither presumptuous in security nor hardened by despair.

D. Augustine's *Biblical exegesis* seems to be fundamentally contradictory. He develops the ideas that he finds in the Bible with a radicalism that leaves room for attacks on the Church. Yet he subordinates every interpretation of the Bible to the authority of the Church, which can discard the Bible when it pleases. The Church alone decides which is the right interpretation. The Bible is the source—then it becomes dangerous to the Church. The Bible is an instrument—then the Church determines the right way to use it. The Bible is to be taken literally; the Bible is to be interpreted according to the spirit.

Nothing is easier than to find contradictions in Augustine. We take them as a feature of his greatness. No philosophy is free from contradictions— and no thinker can aim at contradiction. But Augustine is one of the thinkers who venture into contradictions, who draw their life from the tension of enormous contradictions. He is not one of those who strive from the outset for freedom from contradictions; on the contrary, he lets his thinking run aground on the shoals of contradiction when he tries to think God. Augustine faces the contradictions. And more than that: he presses them to their utmost limits. He makes us aware of the provocative question: Is there a point, a limit, where we are bound to encounter contradiction? And of the answer: Yes, wherever, moved by the source of being and the unconditional will within us, we seek to communicate ourselves in thought, that is to say, in words. In this realm, freedom from contradiction would be existential death and the end of thinking itself. It is because Augustine took up these essential contradictions that he still exerts so provocative a power. And it is because, working with the methods of ecclesiastical thinking, he encompassed a maximum of contradictions—even in opposition to reason—that he was able, within the authority of the Church, to meet its needs so eminently without devising a system.

The disturbing contradictions in Augustine can largely be explained by the different levels of his thinking and so shown to be nonessential. His ecclesiastical thinking; his speculation on freedom based on the Bible and St. Paul (the doctrine of sin and grace); his pure thinking that breaks away from the props of the Bible and the Church—these do not have a common origin. We cannot understand him if we consider everything on the same plane. Sometimes his remarkable memory and the constant presence of the Biblical text enable him to speak too fluently.

5. The Form of the Work

Beginning in 391, Augustine thought in the practice of ecclesiastical life. His thinking is not dispersed, but relates to a center, and this manner of thinking produced the form of his work. His copious writings—sermons, letters, polemics, dogmatic treatises, commentaries on the Bible, confessions —were the product of a dynamic mind taken up with a thousand daily concerns. He thought systematically but never conceived a system to which he could hold fast. He produced no systematic main work to which all the others might be subordinated.

The sharpness of his concepts was developed in struggle. He required new distinctions with which to set forth the meaning of the controversy, to define the hostile positions and his own intention. The atmosphere of these controversies and of the concepts connected with them varies with the theme. The question of human freedom (the Pelagian controversy), the nature of God and transcendence (against the Manichaeans and the Neoplatonists), the nature of the Church (against the Donatists)—each involved different passions. But all are related, because the decisions arrived at in one controversy help to define the others.

Augustine enriched the Latin language: he gave the theological language a new pregnancy, brought new suppleness to its means of expressing the torments and tensions of the innermost soul, the pathos of soaring faith.

6. The Personality

Augustine was motivated by a sincere striving to bare his innermost depths. And yet we do not see the face of a man whose whole self is revealed.

From one point of view, one may say: He is inwardly chaotic, and consequently he desires absolute authority; he has a tendency toward nihilism, and consequently he requires an absolute guarantee; he is without strong attachments in the world (friends, a woman), and consequently he strives for God without a world. Such a psychology of contradictions may be illuminating on one plane, but it does not attain to the earnestness of Augustinian thinking.

Or from a related viewpoint one may say: Thinking of this kind would not have been possible without Augustine's youth; hence it was determined by his early life. His conversion is so essential to many of his ideas that without it they lose their truth. Those who have not experienced such a conversion cannot find a model in Augustine.

The life of one born into the Catholic faith and raised in it from early childhood is bound to be more natural, more tranquil, less problematic than that of Augustine. Thus, among born Catholics, it is only the priest or the monk who can fully perceive Augustine's reality and the radical consequences of his ideas.

In our search for an idea of man that can stand up under embodiment, Augustine represents only *one* possibility. For men whose lives are essentially of one piece, who experience no conversion but perpetually renew the philosophical turn, Augustine represents an opposite. He awakens, but he is not lovable in the same sense as a friend or mentor. He cannot be accepted as a guide to life.

Friendship played a part in his youth; we sense a common ardor at Cassiciacum, where he lived with Monica, his son Adeodatus, and a number of friends. We discern a kind of philosophical community, but there is something strange in Augustine's attitude toward it. For what he was seeking is what he subsequently found in the universal Church. It was not the friendship of a philosophizing in common. For later it becomes perfectly clear that for Augustine friendship had its source in the solitude of self-love before God and was nothing more than a meeting in the common faith. He knew the passion of friendship, not the loyalty. In his subsequently crystallized ecclesiastical faith, friendship is present as a sense of being united in the objective community. But there is loyalty only toward God and the Church; otherwise the individual is alone.

Augustine discloses inhuman traits that are too readily overlooked (I choose the word "inhuman" deliberately; one might also speak of unfeeling behavior toward women or of a cold-hearted trampling on human relations). He himself shows an amazing indifference in describing his dealings with women, and his lack of any sense of guilt is all the more striking in view of his constant self-accusation. When his mother held out the possibility of an advantageous marriage, he simply dismissed the mother of his son, who had been his concubine for years. But his bride-to-be was still a child; while waiting for her to attain a marriageable age, he took another concubine. Speaking of women in retrospect, Augustine is horrified at his sensuality and at his desire for a beautiful wife (*uxor*) belonging to the upper classes. He puts down both these sentiments as worldly lust. One senses that for Augustine as a young man the enjoyment of women was mere habit, that he felt no love for them.

It seems impossible not to regard Augustine's attitude toward his concubines as base, and the same may be said of his calculatingly projected marriage (though every epoch has witnessed such behavior, though there are millions of examples of it today and many persons accept it as a matter of course).

Like certain pagan sects and a few passages in the New Testament, Augustine considered sexuality as such to be evil. He knew an unbridled sensual desire isolated from any higher feeling and later on an ascetic negation of all sensuality. And again it seems impossible not to regard Augustine's dissociation of sexuality from love as unworthy of a human being. Knowing only debauchery and asceticism, he felt no respect for the dignity of women and offended against it in all his relations with them.

He found inspiration only in the love of God. Human simplicity was alien to him. It was replaced by superhuman or inhuman grandeur. He neglected the humanly possible for the sake of the humanly impossible. But this he sought in a never-ending unrest which produced the profound insights and clairvoyant thoughts that make him so great a philosopher.

In his struggle against the pagan faith, Augustine preached the destruction of the divine images. In the year 401 he said at Carthage: It is God's will that the heathen superstition be destroyed. The statues of the gods had been shattered in Rome, and he cried out: "As in Rome, so in Carthage." He stirred up the masses by recalling the early persecutions of Christians. Only this one instance is known to me, but it does not strike me as a matter of indifference that Augustine should even once have been able to participate in the shameful frenzy of fanatical faith (whether pagan or Christian). In any event his step from free persuasion to violent coercion (to his *coge intrare*) was of fundamental importance. In the course of the conflict with the Donatists, he abandoned the lofty humanity of Christian love for the violent enforcement of the unity of the visible Church. And here we find a symptom of the process that was to make Christian love so ambiguous a concept in the eyes of all mankind, particularly outside the confines of the Western world.

As a personality, Augustine is only remotely related to the other great philosophers. In connection with him, one cannot speak of nobility of soul. It is astonishing to find these distasteful traits in a man who showed a unique depth in so many of his thoughts, and it is painful to be unable to dispel a feeling of antipathy.

V. HISTORICAL POSITION, INFLUENCE,
AND PRESENT IMPORTANCE

1. *Historical Position*

Augustine lived during the decline and shortly before the end of the Western Empire. The Roman Empire still existed with its temples and works of art, its rhetoric and philosophy, its public games and theaters.

Africa was a relatively rich province, and Carthage was a large city, rife with luxury. But decay was everywhere. There was no organic solution to the rising discontent (the schismatic Christian Donatists were in league with pillaging rebels, the Circumcelliones), and the Empire lacked the power to withstand the barbarian invaders (the Vandals were besieging Hippo at the time of Augustine's death). Amid the political and economic decline of the Western Roman world, it is as though Augustine, at the last moment, laid the spiritual foundation of an utterly new future. He was the last great figure of Western antiquity. Transforming the past in his work, he passed it on to a new era, in whose spiritual development he played a decisive part.

But this is not how Augustine himself saw it. He did not foresee the end of Western culture. To him Roman culture was both self-evident and indifferent; there was no other. In reading Augustine it is the ancient Roman world, not that of the Middle Ages, that we must bear in mind. Amid increasing distress, mounting violence, and widespread despair, Augustine conceived a courageous attitude with which it was possible to live. It was not meant politically or economically, not based on worldly hopes, but rooted in transcendence and oriented exclusively toward the salvation of the soul in the eternal kingdom of heaven. Thus Augustine, in writing finis to an era, achieved what the philosophers of the preceding centuries had sought and desired and thought they had achieved. But this he did in an entirely different way, as a Christian, rejecting the great, pure, independent philosophy of antiquity. And thus Augustine became the creative thinker who, though he himself did not conceive of anything beyond the ancient world, provided the medieval consciousness amid an entirely different sociological and political reality with its foundation and spiritual weapons. Augustine himself did not live and think within the world-dominating Church of the Middle Ages.

Both as a philosopher and as a Christian, Augustine belonged to an immense tradition. Effective greatness has never risen singly from the void, but is always sustained by a great tradition that sets its tasks. It is new because no one else has done what it succeeds in doing. It is old because it works with materials that were already there, available to all. It is a mistake to exaggerate Augustine's originality, for he is great precisely because of the essentials that he took over from the past; he was sustained by the spiritual whole that was there before him and made up his environment. It is equally wrong to underestimate his originality, for he could not have been foreseen: he melted down the ideas he found and in recasting them breathed new life into them. His original religious experience seems to lend new weight to the traditional doctrines of the Church.

Augustine's spiritual development took on an exemplary character for the West. In a personal form, he embodied a spiritual process extending over several centuries: the transition from independent philosophy to Christian philosophy. In Augustine the forms of ancient philosophy are adapted to a religious thinking grounded in revelation. At the end of an era, at a time when the original impetus of philosophy had long been lost in mere repetition, Augustine, taking the Christian faith as the ground of his philosophizing, seized upon what was then the original possibility. Awakened by the intellectual vitality of pagan philosophy, he brought to Christian thinking his supreme independence. No pagan philosopher of his time or of the following centuries can be mentioned in the same breath with him.

With Augustine the development of dogmatic theology passed from the Orient to the West. The spiritualism of the Eastern Christian thinkers remained a power, but now it was reinforced by realistic practice. In the West, the great tension between negation of the world and accomplishment in the world became a driving force. The world renunciation embodied in monasticism (which spread through the Western world in Augustine's time and which he himself strongly favored) did not paralyze an infinitely patient activity in the world. The intent was still to guide all things toward the eternal kingdom. However, this was to be accomplished not only by secluded meditation but also by practical work in the world. This was the passion of Augustine the ecclesiastic. He created the formulas and arguments that justified this work in the world. This was the beginning of a road that led from the Christian Orient to a steadily increasing activity of many kinds, culminating in the Calvinist ideal of work and worldly asceticism, and finally in a Calvinism shorn of its spiritual content, the empty, meaningless efficiency characteristic of modern life.

2. *Influence*

Augustine was the end of an old tradition in Western Christian thought and the fountainhead of another that has been in progress ever since. His influence seems to be inexhaustible. For through their encounter with him countless philosophers have been awakened to new and original thinking.

His influence springs from two sources, from his originality in which he excels any of the heretics and from his unconditional and unquestioned belief in the authority of the Catholic Church.

It was by his originality that he influenced the heretics. For because Augustine had gathered the widest range of contradictions into his philosophizing, he provided substance for mutually antagonistic parties within the Church and for profound movements of revolt against the Church as well: Gottschalk, the ninth-century monk, Luther, the Jansenists. This first aspect of his thinking provided lasting impulses for a free, original philosophizing. His acceptance of Church authority, on the other hand, gave the Church every right to claim Augustine for its own in nearly all its great spiritual and political struggles. Both lines of influence are well grounded: the first in the particular ideas and movements of thought to which Augustine gave strength, the second in his fundamental and dominant mood.

Augustine represents the unity of the polarities and contradictions inherent in the nature of Christian, Catholic thinking. He seems to provide the foundation of nearly all essential Christian thought, insofar as the great polemical positions of the ensuing centuries took particulars from Augustine but neglected the whole. It has often been possible for each of two contending Christian positions to invoke his authority.

A history of Augustinism would be a history of Christian thought as a whole. If we wish to grasp his essence in order to recognize it in the Christian thinking of later days, we cannot content ourselves with any formula: it is the tendency to original inward thought in contrast to mere intellectual operations; it is a radical thinking-through of problems; it is a thinking grounded in faith, not an intellectual derivation from presupposed dogmas; it is a thinking that follows no prescribed method or system; it is the thinking of the whole man, which in turn makes its claim upon the whole man.

Augustinism enjoyed exclusive dominance down to the twelfth century. The Aristotelianism and Thomism of the thirteenth century brought opposition and completion. But the influence of St. Thomas was limited to the Catholic world. Augustine was no less a force among Protestants than among Catholics.

When we speak of Augustinism in special historical contexts, we are referring to particular doctrines, as, for example, predestination and the corresponding doctrine of grace (Luther, Calvin, the Jansenists) in contrast to the Semipelagianism of the official doctrine; or the "illumination theory of knowledge" in contrast to the Aristotelian theory of abstraction; or the unity of theology and philosophy (the disappearance of philosophy as an independent source) in contrast to the doctrine of degrees, according to which philosophy is an independent field of investigation arched over and completed, but not superseded, by theology.

3. *Augustine's Meaning for Us*

In Augustine, as in scarcely any other thinker, we may study the reality of Christian-Catholic faith (but not of Jesus or of New Testament Christianity). Through him eminently we become acquainted with the fundamental problems that came into the world with Christian thinking. Even if we do not share in such thinking, it is essential that we enter as far as possible into the thoughts of the believer who knows himself to be saved by God's revelation. It is not by the threadbare enlightenment that reduces the Church to a clerical swindle, to wrong thinking and superstition, but by sympathetic study of Augustine's profound themes, by an understanding of this great, authentic opponent, that a philosopher can clarify positions that may be appropriate to his struggle with revealed faith.

Through Augustine we study the themes of Catholicism in their profoundest meaning. He did not know the evil that the Church as a political institution was to bring into the world, more continuously, more consistently, more artfully and ruthlessly than any of the more transient world powers. Through him we can discern at the highest level the eternal opposition that has run through the whole life of the Church: between catholicity and reason, between monolithic authority and the openness of freedom, between the absolute order in the world as the actuality of transcendence and the relative orders in the world as existence with its many compatible possibilities, between cult and free meditation as the center of life, between the outward community of prayer, in which each man shuts himself up in his solitude to find God, and the loneliness before God, which strives to transcend itself in communication with men, through the never-ending process of loving self-fulfillment.

But for us there is something more essential: From Augustine we gain the fundamental positions in our thinking of God and freedom, in the exploration of the soul; and we gain basic operations of thought, which retain their force of conviction even without revealed faith. Through Augustine's thinking we penetrate to that innermost point where the soul transcends itself, the source of speech and guidance, where men can meet as men. Even though Augustine's purpose is to perfect and to justify the soul's absolute solitude before God, we penetrate, through his thinking, to that innermost point. Augustine enables us to participate in his experience of extreme situations, of the hopelessness of worldly existence as such, of the perversions and issuelessness of man's being—and all this is encompassed, not in a rational freedom that seeks its way without guarantee in the mere hope of help if it earnestly does what it can, but in the certainty of grace, guaranteed by ecclesiastical authority and its one exclusive truth. The greatness of Augustine for those who philosophize resides in the fact that the truth he awakens in us is no longer Augustine's Christian truth.

For independent philosophy, thinking with Augustine means: to experience the thematic and existential coincidence of his movements of thought with those of original philosophy. It raises the critical question as to whether, detached from their ground in Christian faith, these movements of thought, though no longer the same, can still be true and effective.

We experience a constant sense of strangeness in dealing with Augustine. Even if in his awareness of God we recognize our own, we find it (unless we merely consider a few pages out of context) in a strange form that repels us and lends a quality of the incredible to something that has just spoken to us from the depths.

Through the grandeur of his thought, Augustine remains the most impressive representative of those who, human themselves, dare to claim that they can instruct others about God, and then go on to cite as their witnesses to an absolute truth men who, as far as we can know, were without exception human beings, no less subject to error than we are. While this claim attests a love of man for man, a joy in sharing his certainty with others, it also discloses unmistakably a will to power, having as its corollary a will to submission, which in the main point has relinquished all striving to think independently.

A strange atmosphere of arrogant humility, of sensual asceticism, of perpetual veiling and reversal, runs through Christianity more than any other faith. Augustine was the first to perceive all this. He knew the torment of inner disharmony, of false and hidden motives—the dogma of original sin made this evil absolute in regard to worldly existence and in a manner of speaking justified it. The self-penetration that set in with Augustine continued down through the Christian thinkers to Pascal, to Kierkegaard and Nietzsche.

BIBLIOGRAPHY

EDITOR'S NOTE

The Bibliography is based on that given in the German original. English translations are given wherever possible. Selected English and American works have been added; these are marked by an asterisk.

Plato

SOURCES:

Platonis Opera, ed. by John Burnet. 5 vols. in 6. Oxford, Clarendon Press, 1902-10.

The Dialogues of Plato, trans. by Benjamin Jowett. 2 vols. New York, Random House, 1937.

Plato, trans. by H. N. Fowler, W. R. M. Lamb, R. G. Bury. (Loeb Classical Library.) 10 vols. London and New York, Wm. Heinemann, Ltd., and G. P. Putnam's Sons, 1919-29.

Plato: *The Republic,* trans. by Paul Shorey. (Loeb Classical Library.) 2 vols. London and New York, Wm. Heinemann, Ltd., and G. P. Putnam's Sons, 1930-35.

Plato: *The Dialogues,* trans. by Floyer Sydenham and Thomas Taylor. 5 vols. London, printed for Thomas Taylor by R. Wilks, 1804.

Plato's dialogues (in roughly chronological order, no certain sequence having been established. English translations other than those listed above are given).

Ion.

Hippias Minor.

Hippias Maior (?).

Protagoras, Benjamin Jowett's trans., rev. by Martin Ostwald, ed. by G. Vlastos. New York, Liberal Arts Press, 1956.

Apology, in *Euthyphro, Apology, Crito and Symposium,* Benjamin Jowett's trans., rev. by Moses Hadas. Chicago, H. Regnery Co., 1953.

Crito, in *Euthyphro, Apology, Crito and Symposium,* Benjamin Jowett's trans., rev. by Moses Hadas. Chicago, H. Regnery Co., 1953.

Laches.

Charmides.

Euthyphro, in *Euthyphro, Apology, Crito and Symposium,* Benjamin Jowett's trans., rev. by Moses Hadas. Chicago, H. Regnery Co., 1953.

Lysis.

Gorgias.

Menexenos.

Meno, in *Protagoras and Meno,* trans. by W. K. C. Guthrie. (Penguin Classics.) Harmondsworth, Penguin Books, 1956.

Euthydemus.

Cratylus.

Phaedo, trans. with introduction and commentary by Reginald Hackforth. Cambridge, Cambridge University Press, 1955.

Symposium, trans. by Walter Hamilton. (Penguin Classics.) London and Baltimore, Penguin Books, 1952.

The Republic, trans. by Francis Macdonald Cornford. New York, Oxford University Press, 1956.

Phaedrus, trans. by Reginald Hackforth. Cambridge, Cambridge University Press, 1952.

Parmenides, in *Plato and Parmenides: Parmenides' Way of Truth and Plato's Parmenides,* trans. with introduction and running commentary by Francis Macdonald Cornford. New York, Liberal Arts Press, 1957.

Theaetetus, in *Plato's Theory of Knowledge: the Theaetetus and the Sophist of Plato,* trans. with running commentary by Francis Macdonald Cornford. (Liberal Arts Library.) London, Routledge and Kegan Paul, 1951.

Sophist, in *Plato's Theory of Knowledge: the Theaetetus and the Sophist of Plato,* trans. with running commentary by Francis Macdonald Cornford. (Liberal Arts Library.) London, Routledge and Kegan Paul, 1951.

Statesman, trans. of *Politicus* by Joseph Bright Skemp. New Haven, Yale University Press, 1952.

Philebus, in *Philebus and Epinomis,* trans. by Alfred Edward Taylor. New York, Thomas Nelson & Sons, 1956.

Timaeus, in *Plato's Cosmology: the Timaeus of Plato,* trans. with running commentary by Francis Macdonald Cornford. New York, Humanities Press, 1957.

Critias.

The Laws, trans. by Alfred Edward Taylor. London, Dent, 1934.

Ast, Friedrich: *Lexicon Platonicum.* 3 vols. Berlin, H. Barsdorf, 1908.

*Abbott, Evelyn: *Subject-index to the Dialogues of Plato.* Oxford, Clarendon Press, 1875.

Plutarch: "Dion," in *The Lives of the Noble Grecians and Romans,* trans. by John Dryden, rev. by Arthur Hugh Clough. New York, Modern Library, 1946.

Diogenes Laertius: *Lives of Eminent Philosophers,* trans. by Robert Drew Hicks. (Loeb Classical Library.) 2 vols. Cambridge, Mass., Harvard University Press; London, Wm. Heinemann, Ltd., 1950.

SECONDARY WORKS:

Apelt, Otto: *Platonische Aufsätze.* Leipzig and Berlin, Teubner, 1912.

*Barker, Ernest: *Greek Political Theory: Plato and His Predecessors.* 5th printing. London, Methuen, 1957.

——: *The Political Thought of Plato and Aristotle.* London, Methuen, 1906.

*Bluck, Richard Stanley Harold: *Plato's Life and Thought.* London, Routledge and Kegan Paul, 1949.

Burnet, John: *Early Greek Philosophy.* New York, Meridian Books, 1957.

*Cherniss, Harold Frederick: *Aristotle's Criticism of Plato and the Academy.* Baltimore, Johns Hopkins Press, 1944.

*Cornford, Francis Macdonald, see above under *Sources* (*The Republic, Parmenides, Theaetetus, Sophist Timaeus*).

Dodds, E. R.: "The Parmenides of Plato and the Origin of the Neoplatonic 'One'," *Classical Quarterly,* XXII (London, 1928), 129-42.

*Else, Gerard F.: "The Terminology of Ideas," *Harvard Studies in Classical Philology,* XLVII (1936), 17-55.

*Foster, Michael Beresford: *The Political Philosophy of Plato and Hegel*. New York, Oxford University Press, 1935.

Frank, Erich: *Plato und die sogenannten Pythagoräer*. Halle, Max Niemeyer, 1923.

Fränkel, Hermann: *Wege und Formen frühgriechischen Denkens*. Munich, Beck, 1955.

Friedländer, Paul: *Plato*, trans. by Hans Meyerhoff. Vol. I. New York, Pantheon Books (Bollingen Series LIX), 1958.

Hoffmann, Ernst: *Platon*. Zurich, Artemis Verlag, 1950.

Jaeger, Werner Wilhelm: *Paideia: the Ideals of Greek Culture*, trans. by Gilbert Highet. 3 vols. New York, Oxford University Press, 1944.

————: *The Theology of the Early Greek Philosophers*, trans. by E. S. Robinson. New York, Oxford University Press, 1947.

Krüger, Gerhard: *Einsicht und Leidenschaft: das Wesen des platonischen Denkens*. Frankfurt am Main, Vittorio Klostermann, 1939.

*Koyré, Alexandre: *Discovering Plato*, trans. by Leonora Cohen Rosenfield. New York, Columbia University Press, 1945.

Leisegang, Hans: "Platon," in Pauly-Wissowa, *Realencyclopädie*. Stuttgart, J. B. Metzler, 1950.

Natorp, Paul: *Platos Ideenlehre: eine Einführung in den Idealismus*. Leipzig, F. Meiner, 1921.

Reidemeister, Kurt: *Das exakte Denken der Griechen: Beiträge zur Deutung von Euklid, Plato, Aristoteles*. Hamburg, Claassen & Goverts, 1949.

*Robinson, Richard: *Plato's Earlier Dialectic*, 2d ed. Oxford, Clarendon Press, 1953.

Ross, Sir William David: *Plato's Theory of Ideas*. New York, Oxford University Press, 1951.

*Shorey, Paul: *Platonism, Ancient and Modern*. Berkeley, University of California Press, 1938.

Stenzel, Julius: *Zahl und Gestalt bei Platon und Aristoteles*. 3d ed. Bad Homburg vor der Höhe, H. Gentner, 1959.

*Stewart, John Alexander: *Plato's Doctrine of Ideas*. Oxford, Clarendon Press, 1909.

*Taylor, Alfred Edward: *Plato: the Man and His Work*. 6th ed. London, Methuen, 1952.

*————: "Forms and Numbers: a Study in Platonic Metaphysics," *Mind* (new series), XXXV (1926), 419-40; XXXVI (1927), 12-33.

Wilamowitz-Moellendorff, Ulrich von: *Platon*. Berlin, Weidemann, 1948.

Wilpert, Paul: *Zwei aristotelische Frühschriften über die Ideenlehre*. Regensburg, J. Habbal, 1949.

Zeller, Eduard: *Outlines of the History of Greek Philosophy*, 13th ed., rev. by Wilhelm Nestle and trans. by L. R. Palmer. New York, Meridian Books, 1955.

Augustine

SOURCES:

Opera Omnia, vols. 32-47 in *Patrologiae cursus completus (Series Latina)*, ed. by Jacques Paul Migne. 221 vols. Paris, 1844-64.

The Works of Aurelius Augustinus, ed. by Marcus Dodds. 15 vols. Edinburgh, T. & T. Clark, 1872-76.

A Select Library of Nicene and Post-Nicene Fathers of the Christian Church, ed. by Philip Schaff. Series I, Vols. 1-8. Buffalo, Christian Literature Company, 1886-88.

Basic Writings, ed. by Whitney J. Oates. 2 vols. New York, Random House, 1948.

Possidius: *Augustins Leben,* German trans. by Adolf von Harnack. Berlin, Verlag der Akademie der Wissenschaften for Walter de Gruyter & Co., 1930. (English trans. in *Possidius,* ed. with rev. text, introduction, and notes by Herbert T. Weiskolten. Princeton, Princeton University Press, 1919.)

SECONDARY WORKS:

Bardy, Gustave: *Saint Augustin, l'homme et l'oeuvre.* 6th ed. Paris, Desclée de Brouwer, 1946.

*Bourke, Vernon Joseph: *Augustine's Court of Wisdom: Life and Philosophy of the Bishop of Hippo.* Milwaukee, Bruce Publishing Company, 1945.

*Burleigh, John Henderson Seafort: *The City of God: a Study of St. Augustine's Philosophy.* London, Nisbet, 1944.

*Cochrane, Charles Norris: *Christianity and Classical Culture: a Study of Thought and Action from Augustus to Augustine.* Rev. ed. New York, Oxford University Press, 1944. See esp. pp. 376-516.

*Figgis, John Neville: *The Political Aspects of St. Augustine's City of God.* London, Longmans, 1921.

*Gilson, Étienne: *History of Christian Philosophy in the Middle Ages,* trans. by Cécile Gilson. New York, Random House, 1955. Part III.

————: *Introduction à l'étude de Saint Augustin,* 2d ed. rev. and enl. Paris, J. Vrim, 1943.

————: *Les Métamorphoses de la Cité de Dieu.* Louvain, Publications universitaires de Louvain, 1952.

*Henry, Paul: "Augustine and Plotinus," *Journal of Theological Studies,* XXXVIII (London, 1937), 1-23.

Holl, Karl: "Augustins innere Entwicklung," in his *Gesammelte Aufsätze zur Kirchengeschichte,* Vol. III. Tübingen, J. C. B. Mohr, 1928.

Jonas, Hans: *Augustin und das paulinische Freiheitsproblem.* Göttingen, Vandenhoeck & Ruprecht, 1930.

Marrou, Henri-Irénée: *Saint-Augustin et la fin de la culture antique.* 2 vols. New enl. ed. Paris, De Boccard, 1949.

Nørregaard, Jens: *Augustins Bekehrung.* Tübingen, J. C. B. Mohr, 1923.

Portalié, E.: "Augustin," in *Dictionnaire de théologie catholique,* Vol. I, cols. 2268-2472. 2d ed. Paris, Letouzey et Ané, 1909.

St. Augustine, by M. C. D'Arcy *et al.* New York, Meridian Books, 1957.

Scholz, Heinrich: *Glaube und Unglaube in der Weltgeschichte: ein Kommentar zur Augustins De Civitate Dei.* Leipzig, J. C. Hinrichs, 1911.

Troeltsch, Ernst: *Augustin, die christliche Antike und das Mittelalter.* Munich, R. Oldenbourg, 1915.

INDEX OF NAMES